ROUTLEDGE LIBRARY EDITIONS: LIBRARY AND INFORMATION SCIENCE

Volume 92

THE SERIALS PARTNERSHIP

THE SERIALS PARTNERSHIP
Teamwork, Technology and Trends:
Proceedings of the North American Serials
Interest Group, Inc.

Edited by
PATRICIA OHL RICE AND JOYCE L. OGBURN

LONDON AND NEW YORK

First published in 1990 by The Haworth Press, Inc.

This edition first published in 2020
by Routledge
2 Park Square, Milton Park, Abingdon, Oxon OX14 4RN

and by Routledge
52 Vanderbilt Avenue, New York, NY 10017

Routledge is an imprint of the Taylor & Francis Group, an informa business

© 1990 The Haworth Press, Inc.

All rights reserved. No part of this book may be reprinted or reproduced or utilised in any form or by any electronic, mechanical, or other means, now known or hereafter invented, including photocopying and recording, or in any information storage or retrieval system, without permission in writing from the publishers.

Trademark notice: Product or corporate names may be trademarks or registered trademarks, and are used only for identification and explanation without intent to infringe.

British Library Cataloguing in Publication Data
A catalogue record for this book is available from the British Library

ISBN: 978-0-367-34616-4 (Set)
ISBN: 978-0-429-34352-0 (Set) (ebk)
ISBN: 978-0-367-40693-6 (Volume 92) (hbk)
ISBN: 978-0-367-40699-8 (Volume 92) (pbk)
ISBN: 978-0-367-80853-2 (Volume 92) (ebk)

Publisher's Note
The publisher has gone to great lengths to ensure the quality of this reprint but points out that some imperfections in the original copies may be apparent.

Disclaimer
The publisher has made every effort to trace copyright holders and would welcome correspondence from those they have been unable to trace.

THE SERIALS PARTNERSHIP:
TEAMWORK, TECHNOLOGY AND TRENDS
Proceedings of the
NORTH AMERICAN SERIALS
INTEREST GROUP, Inc.

**4th Annual Conference
June 3-6, 1989
Scripps College
Claremont, California**

Patricia Ohl Rice
Joyce L. Ogburn
Editors

The Haworth Press
New York • London

The Serials Partnership: Teamwork, Technology and Trends: Proceedings of the North American Serials Interest Group, Inc. has also been published as *The Serials Librarian,* Volume 17, Numbers 3/4 1990.

© 1990 by The Haworth Press, Inc. All rights reserved. No part of this work may be reproduced or utilized in any form or by any means, electronic or mechanical, including photocopying, microfilm and recording, or by any information storage and retrieval system, without permission in writing from the publisher. Printed in the United States of America.

The Haworth Press, Inc., 10 Alice Street, Binghamton, NY 13904-1580
EUROSPAN/Haworth, 3 Henrietta Street, London WC2E 8LU England

Library of Congress Cataloging-in-Publication Data

North American Serials Interest Group. Conference (4th : 1989 : Scripps College)
    The serials partnership : teamwork, technology, and trends : proceedings of the North American Serials Interest Group, Inc., 4th Annual Conference, June 3-6, 1989, Scripps College, Claremont, California / Patricia Ohl Rice, Joyce L. Ogburn, editors.
    P. cm.
    Also published as the Serials librarian, v. 17, nos. 3/4.
    Includes bibliographical references.
    ISBN 0-86656-991-X
    1. Serials control systems—Congresses. 2. Serial publications—Congresses. I. Rice, Patricia Ohl. II. Ogburn, Joyce L. III. Title.
Z692.S5N67   1989
025.3'432—dc20   89-28050
                                                                                                                                       CIP

The Serials Partnership: Teamwork, Technology and Trends

CONTENTS

Introduction   xi

KEYNOTE ADDRESS

Money, Means and Content   1
    Gillian Page

THE PROCESS OF SCHOLARLY COMMUNICATION

The Context of Scholarly Communication   15
    Jack H. Schuster

The Scholarly Communication Process in the Humanities: The Role of the Editor   25
    Richard H. Popkin

Scientific Publication: Science News   33
    Daniel B. Menzel

Publish *and* Perish   35
    Alain L. Hénon

Scholarly Communication and the Role of Libraries: Problems and Possibilities for Accessing Journal Articles   43
    David J. Cohen

CD-ROM IN LIBRARIES: REVOLUTION OR REVOLT?

CD-ROM in Libraries: Access, Trends and Challenges   49
    Karen Sandlin Silverman

Observations on the Use of CD-ROM in Academic Libraries   63
    Joseph A. Michalak

The CD-ROM "Revolution" at Columbia: Year One   69
    Beth Juhl
    Anita Lowry

DEPARTMENT STORES TO BOUTIQUES: HOW MANY SERIALS VENDORS AND WHAT KIND OF SERVICES DOES YOUR LIBRARY NEED?

Determining Which Subscription Agency Services Best Meet Your Needs   81
    N. Bernard "Buzzy" Basch

The Serials Acquisition Partnership   87
    Jane Maddox

Order Consolidation: A Shift to Single Vendor Service   93
    Jan Anderson

We Need Department Store *and* Boutique Serials Vendors   99
    October Ivins

ORGANIZATIONAL RESPONSES TO JOURNAL PRICING ISSUES: PLANS FOR ACTION

Serials Pricing Issues: News from the Field   107
    Deana Astle

Report on the ARL Serials Project   111
    Ann Okerson

A Scientist's Assessment of a Microcosm of the Serials Universe   121
    Paul H. Ribbe

SUMMARY SESSION   143

WORKSHOP SESSION REPORTS

The Commercial Binding Agreement: Partners in Preservation   153
    Tim McAdam

Latest Entry Cataloging As an Option *Sharon Scott*	155
Where Are Serials in Your Organization Chart? *Miriam Palm*	159
Non-Print Serials and Title Waves *Marlene Sue Heroux*	163
Serials Analysis for Budget and Collection Review As Well As Cooperative Development *Dana D'Andraia*	167
Creative Strategies for Serials Management: Current Awareness Services *Rebecca Schwartzkopf*	171
To Bid or Not to Bid: Is It Still a Choice? *Bill Wilmering*	175
Waiting for "Nodough": The Future of Service Charges *Margaret M. Merryman*	179
Serials Automation—Before, During and After *Deborah Sommer*	183
The Subscription Agent and the Integrated Library Systems Vendor: A Marriage Made in Heaven? *Constance L. Foster*	187
The Thor Inventory Ruling: Fact or Fiction? *Margaret McKinley*	191
Fourth Annual NASIG Conference Registrants, Scripps College, June 1989	195
Index	209

Introduction

The North American Serials Interest Group (NASIG) held its Fourth Annual Conference at Scripps College, Claremont, California, from June 3-6, 1989. The theme of this year's conference reflects the partnership existing among those who create, produce, distribute, and manage serials information. The Program Committee of NASIG designed a forum which brought together scholars, publishers, vendors, and librarians to share in discussing issues of common concern.

The keynote address by Gillian Page set the tone of the conference by calling attention to a major concern of all participants, namely serials pricing. She approached this issue from the point of view of the publisher, but as one who is sympathetic to the needs of libraries.

The first panel, moderated by Rebecca Lenzini, addressed the process of scholarly communication. After Jack Schuster's analysis of the academic reward structure, Richard Popkin and Daniel B. Menzel described scholarly communication in the humanities and sciences, respectively. Alain Hénon presented the point of view of the university press publisher, and David Cohen discussed developments in online access to scholarly journal articles.

The second panel was titled "CD-ROM in Libraries: Revolution or Revolt?" Papers included Karen Silverman's discussion of the role of a bibliographic utility in vending CD-ROM products; Joseph Michalak's analysis of technological impact on libraries; and Beth Juhl's study of user reactions to CD-ROM.

October Ivins was moderator and a presenter for the third panel, which addressed two related concerns: differences among types of serials vendors, and whether or not a library should consolidate orders with a single vendor. Buzzy Basch and Jane Maddox contrasted "department store" (large) with "boutique" (small or specialist) vendors, while Jan Anderson and October Ivins discussed vendor selection and analysis.

The final panel dealt with organizational and institutional responses to the current journal pricing crisis. Deana Astle brought attendees up to date on networking activities within the library and publishing communities, Ann Okerson reported on the recently released ARL pricing study, and Paul H. Ribbe presented a model for determining journal worth.

This year's proceedings include a transcript of the summary session, moderated by Kit Kennedy, which featured reaction comments by Vicky Reich and John Tagler.

Conference participants had the opportunity to choose among eleven workshops addressing more practical aspects of serials work. Summaries of all workshops are also included in this volume.

The Fifth Annual NASIG Conference will be held at Brock University, St. Catherines, Ontario, Canada, June 2-5, 1990.

We wish to thank Mary Elizabeth Clack, Vice-President of NASIG, for guiding us through the editorial process. We also gratefully acknowledge the assistance of Maxine Schollenberger and Maria Quintana in preparing the typescript.

P.O.R. and J.L.O.
July 1989

KEYNOTE ADDRESS

Money, Means and Content

Gillian Page

Librarians, subscription agents, publishers, printers, editors, contributors and readers of journals have a common problem. The symptom of the problem is that the cost of acquiring the journals is greater than libraries' acquisition budgets. This paper is an attempt to analyse some of the causes and to suggest some ways forward.

The topics that I will consider are money, which is needed to pay for libraries and journals; means, or how we organize and fund our journal system; and content, or what journals contain.

CONTENT

I start with content, because that is fundamental. It is possible to imagine information systems without print on paper, publishers, or librarians; indeed, many people have tried to do that. But it is not possible to imagine the systems without content. Journals exist because some people want to publish in them and others want to read what they have published. Indeed, it is the success of the journal as a means of carrying information that has led to our present prob-

---

Gillian Page is Director of Pageant Publishing, 5 Turners Wood, London NW11 6TD, England.

© 1990 by The Haworth Press, Inc. All rights reserved.

lems. If the number and size of journals had not grown so rapidly, there might not be a budget problem for libraries, at least in the United States.

Journals exist because of their content. Often they originate because a group of scholars finds the existing journals unsatisfactory as a place to publish their work. Publishers have sometimes assumed that if there is sufficient content to fill a journal there will also be a large enough market to make it economically viable. On the whole, that has worked in the past, but it may not do so in the future. It is clear that the average number of subscribers per journal is smaller now than it was five or ten years ago, and that some journals suffer from a very small subscriber base.

The content of a journal is not random. Papers are submitted because of the journal's scope and reputation. Editors of respectable journals carry out a rigorous screening process which combines the advice of referees with their own sense of the journal's direction. Many journals have high rejection rates, and some return a large proportion of accepted papers to authors for revision. This is one way in which a good journal adds value to its content.

A journal provides subject focus and can even create sub-communities of scholars.[1] We all know that some journals have greater prestige and higher impact factors than others. Within the same subject area journals differentiate themselves by taking various approaches to the same subject area. Differentiation is recognized by readers as well as authors. Many readers are browsers seeking enlightenment rather than a particular piece of information. In a study of journal usage at Loughborough University, browsing accounted for more than half the uses.[2] Browsers go to a journal, not to a particular paper. The imprimatur of a journal adds value to its contents in addition to the value added by editing and refereeing. Proposals to change the information system that ignore the social and intellectual role of the journal and the editing process are unlikely to be welcomed by readers or responsible authors.

Readers demand the journals that are of the greatest interest to them. If the content is trivial, poorly presented, or lies outside their particular range, then they may cancel the subscription. If reputable scholars publish regularly in a journal, then that journal is likely to flourish. A journal that is avoided by authors has nothing to publish and so will fail. I shall return to this theme later.

MONEY

My next topic is money, from two standpoints: first, what happens to the finances of a journal when the number of subscribers or number of pages (extent) changes; and second, our attitudes toward profit.

Changes in Numbers of Subscribers and Extent

The easiest way to demonstrate the effect of changes in the number of subscribers to a journal or the number of pages is with figures. My first example is a quarterly journal of about 400 pages a year, with 800 subscribers, falling to 700, without any other changes (see Table 1). For simplicity the figures ignore advertising, back volume sales and so on. The print numbers might be 1,000 in the first case and 900 in the second; the extra copies are for the editors, for abstracting and indexing services, claims, back volumes sales, and promotion, and because printers do not always deliver the precise number for which they are asked.

If the number of subscribers falls, then the costs of distribution will be lower. The print number can be reduced, but the production cost does not fall pro rata. The typesetting and origination costs will be the same and might account for nearly two-thirds of the total production bill. Modern printing and binding machinery works fast. It does not take long to run off an extra 100 copies; the main time is in setting up the machines. Thus, although the print run is down by 100, or 12 percent, the production cost is reduced by only 3 percent. The costs of mailing and packaging are reduced in proportion to the number of subscribers; however, there is little change in the cost of running the subscription system.

Other costs are unchanged but have to be divided among the smaller number of subscribers. The editor expects to be paid the same sum; promotion costs just as much. The publisher's overheads may even go up as more renewal reminders are sent out and more meetings are held to discuss how to restore the subscriber base.

TABLE 1

Effect of Change in the Number of Subscribers

Specimen Figures for a Quarterly Journal

	800 Subscribers	700 Subscribers	Percent Change
DIRECT COSTS			
Production	16100	15650	-3
Editorial Fees & Expenses	4000	4000	0
Promotion	2500	2500	0
Mailing & Distribution	4250	3900	-8
Editorial Board Meeting	1250	1250	0
TOTAL	28100	27300	-3
DIRECT COSTS PER SUBSCRIBER	35.13	39.00	11.03
PUBLISHERS' OVERHEADS	12100	11800	-2
OVERHEADS PER SUBSCRIBER	15.13	16.86	11.45
TOTAL COSTS	40200	39100	-3
TOTAL COSTS PER SUBSCRIBER	50.25	55.86	11.16

The consequence of a decrease of 100 subscribers for this journal is an increase in the total cost per subscriber of over 11 percent. That is why publishers are perturbed by declining sales, and why declines are a major factor in the increase in journal prices. If the subscribers had instead increased from 700 to 800, the cost per subscriber would fall by about 10 percent. The cost of an extra 100 subscribers is only $1,100, or $11 per subscriber.

Now let us see what happens if the number of pages is increased by 10 percent (Table 2). Production, editorial and postage costs will

TABLE 2

Effect of Change in the Number of Pages

Specimen Figures for a Quarterly Journal with 800 Paid Subscribers

	400 Pages	440 Pages	Percent Change
DIRECT COSTS			
Production	16100	17700	10
Editorial Fees & Expenses	4000	4400	10
Promotion	2500	2500	0
Mailing & Distribution	4250	4420	4
Editorial Board Meeting	1250	1250	0
TOTAL	28100	30270	8
DIRECT COSTS PER SUBSCRIBER	35.13	37.84	7.72
PUBLISHERS' OVERHEADS	12100	12300	2
OVERHEADS PER SUBSCRIBER	15.13	15.38	1.65
TOTAL COSTS	40200	42570	6
TOTAL COSTS PER SUBSCRIBER	50.25	53.21	5.90

go up more or less pro rata, but most other costs will be unchanged. Thus we can give the subscriber 10 percent more pages for an increase of only 6 percent in costs.

What do we learn from these figures? First, that similar journals with the same number of pages may have very different finances, depending upon the number of subscribers. Even if some subscribers are paying reduced membership or individual subscription rates, the larger circulation journal can have a lower price and still be more profitable. If the journal carries advertising, the larger circulation may also help to increase income from advertisements, further reducing the per copy costs for subscribers. At the same time, the larger the circulation, the more likely the journal is to be cited, increasing its "impact factor." That is why journals with a low price per page tend to have a higher impact factor than those with a high price per page.[3]

Secondly, we learn that the more pages a journal publishes (within reasonable limits), the better value it can offer for the same number of subscribers. Third, anything that reduces the number of journal subscriptions is bad news both for the publisher and the remaining subscribers. All of these points will come up later on.

Profit

The second aspect of money that I want to consider is profit. Some current comment on journal publishing suggests that the library community is worried by the level of profit in publishing, or in extreme cases, doubtful that publishers should make profits at all. In fact, overall, publishing is not particularly profitable; in the United Kingdom, the average return on sales is 8.6 percent, which is lower than for most other business sectors. There are no great barriers to entry; if publishing were very profitable, one might expect many new firms to start up.

We have first to distinguish between gross profit, which is the difference between the income and the cost of sales (direct costs), and net profit. The library equivalent of a publisher's gross profit is the total library budget less what is spent on acquisitions. Sometimes librarians are astonished by the gross profits of publishers; equally, publishers are amazed that libraries should spend so much on things other than publications. These are two sides of the same coin. People and buildings and organizations cost money.

Net profit is what is left after paying overheads, investment in equipment, interest on borrowed money, and so on. In a not-for-profit organization it is called a surplus, but the principle is the same. A business that does not make one or the other is unlikely to survive for long, since it generates no funds for development or growth. If publishers are to produce innovations such as ADONIS, CD-ROM, or online versions, they have to make profits to pay for them. Of course, some of the profit of commercial firms is usually distributed to stockholders. Not-for-profit concerns have no stockholders, but since their parent societies may expect them to produce a surplus to underwrite non-publishing activities, the net effect is much the same.

Profit is a measure of efficiency. We can imagine two publishers whose journals are identical in every respect, including price, extent, and numbers of subscribers. Publisher A by being efficient makes a handsome profit; publisher B is mismanaged and suffers a loss. Because publisher A is efficient, routines run smoothly, and customers are provided with excellent service. Publisher B is in a mess: potential profits are spent on tidying up the confusion caused by inefficiency. If I were a librarian, I would prefer my suppliers to be profitable type A publishers rather than non-surplus generating B's.

If two journals have markedly different prices per page, and the same number of words on the page, it does not follow that the more expensive is the more profitable. A journal may be cheaper because it has more pages or a more efficient publisher. A not-for-profit publisher may benefit from page charges, tax advantages, or hidden support from other institutions. A journal that gives little or no discount to subscription agents will have a lower cover price than one that does. One journal may have relatively straightforward text; the other may involve much more skilled typesetting. The publishers may employ different methods of allocating internal costs. The more expensive journal may have failed to live up to the editors' and publishers' expectations of the market, but still be able to exist on a smaller circulation with the higher price. Editors or their employing institutions may demand a high sum for editorial expenses. In short, one cannot judge the level of profit from the price.

There is sometimes a faint suggestion that if only all journal publishing were in the hands of not-for-profit publishers, journals would be cheaper. I think this arises from a serious misunderstanding of the economics of journal publishing. It is necessary to compare like with like. Not-for-profit journals that lack a large member subscriber base and do not benefit from volunteer support (such as translation journals) can cost as much as their commercial counterparts. Commercial journals would be cheaper if they enjoyed the benefit of large sales at reduced rates to individuals that learned society publications have. An extension of page charges to all categories of journals worldwide might help, also. But I cannot see any way of bringing this about.

Complaints about publishers' profits are, I believe, misplaced. The real question is whether the price of a particular journal is reasonable. A very expensive journal may be making a loss and a cheaper one a large profit. We do not select our grocery store because of its profits but on grounds of price, quality, convenience, range of goods, and service. The same criteria should apply to buying journals. The catch is that publishers have a monopoly on publishing the journals that they own, and the content of one journal is not a satisfactory substitute for another. I shall return to this later.

MEANS

My third topic is means: first, the means by which journal contents get to readers; and second, the means of finding the funds to support the journal system. When full text online first became a practical proposition, publishers were enthusiastic; apart from the possibilities for improved service to readers, they anticipated increased income. Many librarians see the potential benefits and hope that online journals will reduce their costs, but publishers' keenness has waned.

One reason is economics. Let us assume that our journal with 800 subscribers is offered in full text online and, in consequence, 100 libraries cancel their subscriptions to the print version. At the moment, if the publisher is lucky, the income from online use might cover the cost of making the journal available in digital format. Online use is not contributing anything to the origination cost of the journal. Consequently, the publisher will need to increase the price of the printed version by more than 11 percent in order to stay in the same financial position. Online is only economically viable if the combined income from online and printed versions is greater than the cost of printing plus the cost of mounting the online version.

For the library, work done at Loughborough University suggests that electronic access would have to cost less than about $2 per article (including library overheads) to be competitive with printed versions.[4] At that price, the known demand for specific articles could be filled, but nothing could be done about browsing, which accounted for more than half of the journal uses. Their best online alternative was to buy a core collection of printed journals and to obtain the rest electronically. That way, the library could meet 80 percent of known browsing needs but would leave about 10 percent of current demand unsatisfied.

Online journals will not solve the funding problem for either libraries or publishers. Even if all U.S. libraries went totally online for their journal needs, publishers would still have to produce printed versions for many overseas markets which lack the necessary communication facilities or enthusiasm for reading a foreign language from a screen.

Finding the Funds

The second sort of means that I want to discuss is funding for the information system. Learned journals are the primary source of authoritative publications in their subjects. Journals make available the best work in a field to anyone who wants the information, regardless of where they may live or how many years hence they may want that information. Without publication, what is the use of academic (as distinct from commercial or defence) research? If granting agencies are right, a reasonable proportion of research projects should yield useful or publishable results. Of course, not all research is productive; if the results of the research are trivial it is better for the work not to be published than to clutter up the literature.

Compared with the cost of doing research, the cost of publication is very small. The Publishers Association/ALPSP survey of trends in journal subscriptions for 1987 recorded an average price per editorial page of 15.53 pence, or about 25 cents.[5] If we assume an average article to be 10 pages long, then the cost per article was about $2.50. Since the average number of subscribers per journal was just over 1,000, the cost of publishing an average article was less than $2,500. In fact, that figure is an overestimate, since more than 30 percent of the subscribers got reduced rates, mostly as members of sponsoring societies. I have no figures for the average cost of research, but it is likely that the total cost of getting the permanent record to libraries worldwide is less than 2 percent of the cost of the research.

How can we get across the message that academic research is valueless unless published and that it costs so little extra to make the results of research available? If society has to choose between more research and less information on what research has already been done, versus less new research and more information, then choosing more information will be preferable. How can we persuade the grant givers and funds managers that the library is a vital and cost-effective resource, a point of entry to a high proportion of all the worthwhile research that has ever been done? Can librarians, publishers, subscription agents, journal editors and the academic community work together to create a climate in which the need for and the costs of information are better understood?

Publishers are spending large sums of money worldwide to sell their journals. Many of these efforts are unsuccessful, not because there is no demand for the journals, but because there is no money to pay for them. Perhaps it would be more effective if some of the publicity budget were devoted to creating a climate in which more funds were available for libraries.

The problem is worldwide. If libraries outside the United States had more funds for the purchase of journals, then the increased circulation should lead to lower prices. That in turn would benefit U.S. libraries. The position in the U.S. has been exacerbated by the decline of the dollar relative to other currencies (though that is now changing), but the same problem afflicts many developing countries. In Indonesia, for instance, the libraries of some major institutions can afford only a half dozen journals at most. The World Bank has been spending millions of dollars there on new university libraries, library systems, and book purchases, with token sums for journals. One project allocated $2.3 million for the acquisition of books and only $75,000 for journals, partly because journals do not fit neatly into World Bank tendering systems. Our consciousness-raising efforts should be international.

Before we present our case, are we sure that the costs of the system are reasonable? Librarians may find it hard to believe, but journal prices would be even higher if printers and publishers had not found ways of keeping production cost increases below inflation. Publishers and subscription agents have worked together so that orders and other information can be transmitted between them electronically with significant cost savings, particularly in the entering of orders. Libraries have introduced automation to help keep their costs down. But it seems likely that the prices of journals will rise by more than inflation, at least in the short term.[6,7]

What else can be done? There are still a great many new journals coming on the market. There are many reasons for this. Groups of people taking a particular approach to a subject believe it would be good to have a journal reflecting their interests. Because of the publish or perish syndrome, there are plenty of contributions on offer. Publishers who have seen the sales of their existing journals decline are happy to take on new journals to compensate for their lost sales. Some may fail, or may need high prices to survive, but some may turn into winners.

Publishers have surely noted librarians' complaints about high journal prices. But they have also observed that usually enough libraries are willing to pay whatever subscription price is necessary to cover the costs of an established journal. At the same time, the editors of expensive journals are just as convinced as editors of lower-price ones that their journals are a service to scholarship. They can claim the support of a distinguished editorial board and cite excellent papers that they have published. Should the publisher decide to close such a journal down on the grounds that the economic price distresses librarians? Such an announcement would cause the editors and authors to rise up against the publisher and create an academic scandal. It certainly would not help the publisher acquire books or journals on the same subject in the future.

If librarians are serious about keeping average journal prices per page or per article down, then they have to vote with their wallets. That, it seems to me, is the only place the chain can be broken. If it is clear that there are not going to be enough subscribers to support the journal at any price, a publisher will decide not to take the risk.

At the same time, can librarians do more to educate library users and researchers? These are the people who produce the content of the journals which—because of that content—libraries are obliged to purchase. If enough academics in the institutions represented in

NASIG decided not to write for the journals that librarians find poor value for money, there would be even less reason for subscribing. Universities and research institutions employ not only contributors, but also the present and future editors of these very high-priced journals. Do the editors know how librarians regard these journals and their publishers? Do the editors know what sort of price levels librarians regard as beyond the pale and which they regard as acceptable? If, in spite of this information, academics continue to patronise the journals that you as librarians object to, can they accept the consequences of this life-style and find the funds that will enable libraries to pay for subscriptions?

CONCLUSION

Where has this led us? I believe that journals are and will continue to be a vital tool for the academic community. We need a lively, efficient and profitable (or, if you prefer, surplus-generating) publishing industry that can respond to the needs of authors, readers, and libraries.

Accusations of profiteering may be false and certainly miss the main point: the price is too high for the purchaser. Journals respond to market forces. Libraries' buying habits may have led publishers to believe that high-price small circulation journals are more acceptable than they really are. Perhaps we need more mergers among smaller journals. Publishers have felt the pressure to expand their journal lists and to build up turnover, and scholars have been happy to participate in new journals.

If a journal is unprofitable, a publisher's natural response is to increase the price; experience has shown that few subscriptions are lost by so doing. If librarians want cheaper journals, they should refuse to purchase those they and the library users consider poor value for money. Unless they do that, publishers will continue to respond to the demand from the supply side—the scientists and academics who write the papers—and start new journals.

Finally comes the point that I regard as the most important. We need to work together to see that the journal system is properly run and sufficiently flexible to meet new needs, and that it is properly funded, so that the valuable results of often costly research are available worldwide at a reasonable price.

Last, a note about the title. What Corin the shepherd actually says in *As You Like It* is: "He that wants [lacks] money, means and content [happiness] is without three good friends." Maybe if we can join together as good friends in our determination to support the journal we shall not want for money, means or content in either pronunciation.

NOTES

1. Bryan Coles, "The Intrinsic Value," in *The Changing Market for Serials* (Letchworth, Epsilon Press, 1987).

2. A. F. MacDougall, et al. "Modelling of Journal Versus Article Acquisition: An Evaluation of Different Kinds of Journal Provision by Libraries in the Light of the Possibilities Offered by Electronic Transmission of Journal Articles" (British Library BNB Research Fund, 1985).

3. H. H. Barshall and J. P. Arrington, "The Cost of Physics Journals: A Survey," *Bulletin of the American Physical Society* 33 (1988): 1437-47.

4. A. F. MacDougall et al.

5. Priscilla Oakeshott, "Trends in Journal Subscriptions 1987" (London, Publishers Association, 1988).

6. Gillian Page, "The Next Ten Years—Journal Publishing," in *Serials 87, Proceedings of the UK Serials Group* (Oxford, 1987).

7. Gillian Page, *Journal Publishing* (London and Boston, Butterworths, 1987).

THE PROCESS OF SCHOLARLY COMMUNICATION

The Context of Scholarly Communication

Jack H. Schuster

The process of scholarly communication can be understood only in the context within which communication among scholars originates: the world of higher education and the academic profession. The processes leading to scholarly publication are embedded in a complex network of institutions, personal and professional values, incentives, technologies, and resources. That is to say, scholars, just as any other occupational group, order their priorities and accomplish (or fail to accomplish) their objectives within an environment of motivations, opportunities, and constraints. More to the point, the environment for academics has been undergoing rapid and accelerating change, and those changes have far-reaching consequences for how the process of scholarly communication is triggered and fulfilled. It is a process which, in all its variegated forms, culminates a million and more times each year in published scholarship.

This is not to suggest that the initiation of scholarly communica-

Jack H. Schuster is Professor of Education and Public Policy and head of the graduate program in higher education at The Claremont Graduate School, Harper Hall, 150 E. Tenth Avenue, Claremont, CA 91711-6160.

© 1990 by The Haworth Press, Inc. All rights reserved.

tion is limited to the domain of the academic profession. Nor is published scholarship the only means of "scholarly communication." But the written word, however disseminated or retrieved, is by far the dominant, albeit not exclusive mode, of scholarly communication, and the academic profession accounts for a very large proportion of what can properly be labeled "scholarly writing." That is why the environment of academic scholars must be understood if we seek to comprehend the processes of scholarly communication or endeavor to speculate knowledgeably about what the future may hold.

My observations derive from research begun in 1983 on a study of the American professoriate which was initiated by my senior colleague, Professor Howard R. Bowen. That investigation explored the changing characteristics of faculty members, the quality of their work environment, how they spend their time (including their research and publication activities), the changing reward system in the academy, and projections about the academic labor market.

Apart from that study, which led to the publication in 1986 of the book *American Professors*, I have visited campuses and interviewed faculty members as a part of six other foundation-supported studies. In all, my views about the context in which scholarly communication originates are informed both by extensive field experience — in particular, interviews with hundreds of faculty members and academic administrators concerning the changing conditions of academic life — and by examination of the literature on the academic profession.

With that by way of backdrop, this paper will touch on three topics: first, the escalating trend toward academic specialization; second, the increasing pressures that propel faculty members to publish; and third, anticipated changes in the academic labor market and their implications for scholarly communication.

THE MOMENTUM OF SPECIALIZATION

The accelerating pace of academic specialization is a phenomenon that has been underway for centuries, but most markedly over the past hundred years. In the United States the academic career had become more or less professionalized by the 1880s.[1] As early as 1900, the process of specialization and dispersion among fields was so well advanced that the proponents of general and liberal education "overwhelmed by wave after wave of specialists . . . had already lost the main battle."[2] By that time specialization in teaching and research was in ascendancy, thereby consigning the academic generalist to peripheral significance and making inevitable all the trappings of academic specialization which today dominate higher education's structures, processes, and values. These indicia include academic departments, graduate schools, semi-autonomous research units, discipline-based learned societies, specialized journals, and, ultimately, "the rapid decline in teaching loads for productive scholars."[3]

It is the "end product" of that massive and complicated system which serial librarians are perhaps uniquely positioned to observe. More than observe, of course, they must somehow cope with the proliferation of periodicals and other publications spewed forth by legions of scholars.

We all are acutely aware of the exponential increase in the number of titles that address subfields that were barely coalescing or were even totally uninvented a few decades, or just a few years, ago. The profusion of titles and of learned societies both symbolizes and reflects the process by which specialization begets subspecialization, which in turn begets sub-subspecialization—and on and on. As noted, the development of specialized knowledge has been going on for a very long time, in some respects, of course, spanning the millenia. But only in recent decades has the rate of expansion become explosive.

This is not the time to dwell on the awesome statistics of proliferation and fragmentation, but a few data will help to underscore the point. Exhibit A, for example, could be the current edition of *Ulrich's International Periodicals Directory* (1988-89) with its list of 108,590 titles. In vivid contrast, the comparable figure for 1969-70 was just half that amount: 54,500.[4] Put another way, the current listing works out to one periodical for every four-and-a-half full-time American faculty members. Or consider the rate of scholarly production. Academics in the sciences, according to one recent estimate, produce articles for 40,000 separate journals at the frenzied pace of almost 3,000 each and every twenty-four hour period—which is to say two articles every minute of every hour.[5] (Did I hear someone say he was having a hard time keeping up with reading in his field?)

Regarding the fragmentation of disciplinary associations or learned societies, a few comments will have to suffice. For one thing, the larger, "general interest" associations of scholars are being cannibalized, in effect, by smaller, more narrowly targeted associations. Thus, such fixtures of higher learning as the American Association for the Advancement of Science (founded in 1848) and the American Physical Society (1899) have seen their memberships and conference attendance drop off sharply. Clark makes the point that they are victims of "splinteritis."[6] In their stead have arisen large numbers of focused national and regional associations. Clark notes that "Among the [367 national] associations operating in 1985, two-thirds had originated since 1940, with 150 [or 41 percent] starting up after 1960."[7]

In all, the momentum toward academic specialization and fragmentation is powerful, irreversible, and shapes profoundly the environment in which academics go about the business of conducting research and disseminating their findings.

THE MANDATE TO PUBLISH

As indicated above, academics account for a tremendous amount of "scholarly communication." Although somewhere between a third and a half of all faculty members in four-year colleges and universities do little or no publishing, those who do publish, all together, generate a massive output.[8] It is not difficult to establish that the quantity of scholarly publishing has escalated sharply. Nor is it very difficult to understand why that has happened. The basic difference is that today more and more institutions expect their faculty members to publish and, accordingly, reward systems for academics are more tightly linked to demonstrated scholarship and published results. Several aspects of the shifting reward system bear mentioning.

Junior Faculty

Efforts by junior faculty members to obtain tenure is one factor that contributes to the outpouring of publications. More precisely, it is the *perception* that it has become more difficult to attain tenured status that drives junior faculty members to publish more. I make the distinction between the *reality* of earning tenure and the *perception* of what it takes for two reasons.

First, there are no reliable data on the rates at which tenure is successfully attained.[9] For one thing, even if the number of favorable and unfavorable decisions were made available campus by campus, those data would ignore how many faculty members were counseled out prior to a formal decision or how many departed on their own volition after sizing up a tough situation. Thus, beyond knowing that more full-time faculty members than ever before are tenured—somewhere between 67 and 70 percent—the facts about obtaining tenure are in short supply.

Second, I am acquainted with quite a few instances of misperceptions, that is, campuses where a virtually universal perception obtains that tenure has become more difficult to achieve despite the evidence that tenure-earning rates on campus, in fact, are the same or even higher than they had been. I conclude that tenure almost certainly is more difficult to come by at many campuses, but probably not as difficult as is widely thought to be the case. Nonetheless, perceptions are the key element.

Mid-Career and Senior Faculty

The imperative to publish also grips mid-career academics more tightly than in times past. Thus, tenured associate professors at many campuses are being told explicitly that to earn a promotion will require publications. The same applies, in many instances, for full professors seeking step promotions. Indeed, publication rates do not appear to diminish with attainment of the highest academic rank. Extrinsic rewards—for instance, job security, rank, and compensation—do not alone shape motivations to publish. As summarized in one comprehensive review of the literature on scholarly productivity, "Publication does not stop when the incentive provided by the prospect of promotion is no longer operative, but rather seems to increase, and this [finding] supports . . . the preeminent role of 'intrinsic' as opposed to 'extrinsic' motives for research involvement."[10]

The publishing imperative has not altered significantly at the research universities,[11] nor has the essentially exclusive emphasis on teaching, rather than research, diminished at the community colleges. But at many—I would guess most—of the two thousand or so four-year liberal arts colleges and comprehensive colleges and universities, an increasing emphasis on research is manifest.

Additional Indicators

There are a number of symptoms of this exaggerated mandate to publish. One indicator is the evidence of scientific fraud, of faked experimental results. I cannot say whether such cheating has actually increased proportionate to the total amount of research activity, but a number of shocking incidents of fraud have been brought to light in recent years.

There are other indicators. A recent editorial on scientific fraud in the *Journal of Medical Education* makes the point:

> One strategy that appears to have been frequently adopted for meeting perceived requirements for scientific productivity is to divide the publication of a coherent research result into multiple fragments and thus to create the impression of a more prolific record of accomplishment than is warranted.[12]

The author goes on to discuss the consequent problems of multiple and "honorary" authorship. That is, especially in the sciences, there appear to be more-and-more instances of article coauthorship being extended to colleagues or associates who may have had little or nothing to do with, and, accordingly, no responsibility for, the published research. Presumably such favors are returned in kind by grateful beneficiaries, and the resulting bloated curricula vitae no doubt dazzle more than a few promotion and tenure committees. The practice of scholars who list their names (or permit the listing of their names) as coauthors of works actually written by others is not ethical. "This practice," writes Cahn, "while customary in certain fields, is blatantly dishonest."[13] But the reasons for such conduct are not mysterious.

In fact, I now lay claim to having discovered Schuster's Law which for the first time takes into account the vectors of article fragmentation and multiple authorship. This Law of Contemporary Academic Life holds that the space required to list authors is increasing relative to the length of the material published at such a rapid rate that by the year 2018, authorship credits will be longer than the accompanying article in 34 percent of all published articles. Remember, you heard it here first, and I can hardly wait to publish these results—just as soon as I can cut a mutual coauthorship deal with several of my colleagues!

The Influence of Supply and Demand

What has changed significantly is the academic labor market. Over the past two decades the market has flip-flopped from a strong sellers' market that prevailed during the latter part of the 1950s and 1960s—that is, the sellers of academic talent (individual professors)—to a strong buyers' market that has been in ascendancy since the early 1970s. In almost all academic fields, the hiring institutions found themselves able to take advantage of a favorable supply-demand imbalance and have been able to hire well-trained, research-oriented new faculty members. Most institutions reported that they have been able to appoint the best faculty members their respective campuses have ever employed.[14] These developments have been accompanied by the ageless ambition to emulate the most renowned research universities. Thus, to sum up this point, colleges and universities have been in a position to hire well, they have been able to demand scholarly production, and they have not hesitated to do so.

In all, the pressures to publish—both extrinsic and intrinsic, for faculty of all ranks, and at most institutions—are formidable. Taken together with the first topic—the rapid growth of subspecialties and the spiraling number of periodicals on standby to receive and report the results—one finds ample explanation for the deluge of scholarly publications.

SOME ANTICIPATED CHANGES

My final point speculates about the consequences for scholarly communication of anticipated changes in the environment of higher education, in particular, the academic labor market. It is now widely assumed that the increased demand for academic talent will begin to outrun the supply of prospective faculty members in many fields by the mid 1990s.

As academe begins to grapple with the problem of how to make some 430,000 new faculty appointments over the next two decades, some important things will change.[15] Faculty members will rejoice in the rebirth of the late lamented sellers' market. Institutions of higher education will not be able to exert as much leverage over individual faculty members. They will presumably not be able to demand quite as much by way of scholarly publication. Simultaneously, I believe that new definitions of "scholarship" are being evolved that will acknowledge professors' scholarly activities that may stop short of traditional publication. Still further, there has been a resurgence in recent years, appropriately so, in the emphasis on undergraduate teaching, and this trend may be exerting a slight counterbalance to institutional pressures to publish, enabling faculty members at some institutions to pay less attention to publication as the predominant criterion for professional advancement.

On the other hand, I do not anticipate that the current outpourings of publications will be stanched by changes in market conditions or the rediscovery that undergraduate teaching has been neglected. Emerging technologies and some that have not yet surfaced undoubtedly will alter radically important aspects of scholarly communication, and these new modes almost certainly will make much easier some forms of communication at a time when skyrocketing costs per unit will constrain traditional modes of publication.

Whatever the technological future may hold, the forces of specialization and the incentives to publish will almost certainly overwhelm any tendencies to lessen scholarly production. Publications, in whatever form, will not be displaced as the coin of the academic realm.

The result will be an avalanche of publications and an increasing need for super-strength headache remedies for many NASIG members. I wish you well!

NOTES

1. Laurence R. Veysey. *The Emergence of the American University* (Chicago: University of Chicago Press, 1965); Christopher Jencks and David Riesman. *The Academic Revolution* (Garden City, N.Y.: Doubleday, 1968).
2. Burton R. Clark. *Academic Life: Small Worlds, Different Worlds* (Princeton: Carnegie Foundation for the Advancement of Teaching, 1987).
3. Jencks and Riesman, *The Academic Revolution*, 15.
4. The 1988-89 edition of *Ulrich's International Periodicals Directory* (New York: R. R. Bowker) combines for the first time listings for regular and irregular serials. The combined listings for the two separate volumes (*Ulrich's* and Ulrich's *Irregular Serials and Annuals: An International Directory*) for 1969-70 covered 54,500 titles. By the time the 1979-80 volumes were issued, the number of listings had mushroomed to 94,500.
5. Michael J. Maloney, "Scientific Publication and Knowledge Politics," *Journal of Social Behavior and Personality*, 2 no. 2 [pt. 1] (1987), cited in Charles J. Sykes, *Profscam* (Washington, D.C.: Regnery Gateway, 1988), 115.
6. Clark, *Academic Life*, 234.
7. Clark, *Academic Life*, 37.
8. Martin J. Finkelstein. *The American Academic Profession: A Synthesis of Social Scientific Inquiry Since World War II* (Columbus, Ohio: Ohio State University Press, 1984).
9. Dolores L. Burke. *A New Academic Labor Marketplace* (New York: Greenwood Press, 1988).
10. Finkelstein, *The American Academic Profession*, 101.
11. Clark Kerr. *The Uses of the University*, 3rd ed. (Cambridge, Mass.: Harvard University Press, 1982).
12. Thomas J. Kennedy Jr. "Scientific Fraud," *Journal of Medical Education* 63 (1988): 806-08.
13. Steven M. Cahn. *Saints and Scamps: Ethics in Academe* (Totowa, N.J.: Rowman and Littlefield, 1986), 44.
14. Howard R. Bowen and Jack H. Schuster. *American Professors: A National Resource Imperiled* (New York: Oxford University Press, 1986).
15. Bowen and Schuster, *American Professors*.

The Scholarly Communication Process in the Humanities: The Role of the Editor

Richard H. Popkin

Because my expertise is limited to the humanities, and more specifically to philosophy and intellectual history, my discussion will be from this perspective.

The scholarly communication process in the humanities goes on at a much slower and more leisurely pace than in the sciences and social sciences. Authors work out their ideas in tentative ways, often first proposing them to colleagues, to correspondents, and as presentations at colloquia, seminars, and professional meetings. The feedback from these initial proposals (which are probably somewhat accelerated nowadays by BITNET and FAX machines) can last months and years. The product submitted to a learned journal may bear little resemblance to the initial formulation.

In contrast, there are some scholars who believe that their communication has to go directly from the typewriter or the word processor to a learned publication. The result of this haste is all too often almost instantaneous rejection.

The role of the editor begins either with an unsolicited submission, presumably digested through discussions, correspondences and informal critiques; or with solicited material. Let me first say something about the latter, before dealing with the trickier problems involved in the former. Part of an editor's job is to make her or his journal interesting, informative, and a source for new and/or impor-

Richard H. Popkin is President, *Journal of the History of Philosophy*, and Adjunct Professor, Department of History, University of California, 405 Hilgard Avenue, Los Angeles, CA 90024-1473.

© 1990 by The Haworth Press, Inc. All rights reserved.

tant presentations and discussions. Often some of these objectives are accomplished by soliciting articles, discussions and book reviews either from people established as experts and/or creative scholars, or from people who are working on something new and exciting who, for many psychological reasons, have not yet seen fit to submit their work to a scholarly publication. The editor in these cases has to be aware of the experts in many sub-fields, and has to keep abreast of ongoing informal discussions, and even private ones.

For better or worse, there are people who are so diffident they do not believe that what they have been working on, sometimes for years and years, is yet ready to show formally to the world of learning. I know cases of people who have worked and worked on manuscripts, constantly making revisions, or rethinking the material. Then through the efforts of an editor, the item is pried from them, and contributed to the scholarly world.

The solicited material is usually published with slight revisions, unless it is incomplete, or libelous, or obscene. In these cases it can become a quite sticky matter, since the solicitation almost constitutes a compact to publish. The editor, if he or she feels strongly, can request changes, and even leave the manuscript in limbo until the author gets sufficiently annoyed and withdraws it. I know of some cases where the editor just put the item in a drawer and never answered mail from the author. The author passed away, and the contribution just sits in suspended animation, perhaps to be lost forever.

An interesting case, not exactly fitting the above circumstances, is that of the English philosopher, John Locke, who asked his friend Sir Isaac Newton why he did not believe in the Doctrine of the Trinity. He asked Newton to write out his reasons for publication in the journal of a friend of Locke's in Holland, Jean LeClerc. Newton wrote two letters and sent them to Locke, who raised some points, mainly asking Newton for more details from the then important Bible scholars. The final version was put together and sent on to Holland. Newton and Locke decided that, since Newton's views on the matter were so heretical, the letters ought to be published anonymously. LeClerc began the physical process of publishing the letters. They were translated and put in form for the printer. At this point, Newton panicked. He feared that people would recognize him to be the author, and that he would then lose all of his positions and perquisites, since he obviously did not subscribe to the Thirty-nine Articles of the Church of England. The letters were laid aside and only surfaced when the editor LeClerc passed away. They were found in LeClerc's papers and printed for the first time twenty-five years after Newton's death. A third letter, giving the strongest support to Newton's heresies, only surfaced in the 1960s when Newton's correspondence was published. Now, when the theological issue is not so agitating, one can calmly look at Newton's publications. But they are not now, as they were originally intended to be, part of lively discussion which was all-important to the participants. Instead they are now historical curiosities about what a great man thought years ago.

The bulk of scholarly communication in the humanities is unsolicited. People submit their manuscripts, usually, as indicated, after a good deal of incubation. The editor's first job is to ascertain as quickly as possible whether the submission is within the purview of the journal, and if it qualitatively can be considered. If so, then it is becoming the case (and I am not sure it is all for the best), that the submission is sent to referees, usually two. In the last two decades this process has become blind, that is, the referees do not know who the author is. It is the editor's responsibility to find good referees. This is not as easy as it might sound, since in the humanities it is often difficult to find so-called "objective standards." (Some recent discussions indicate that similar problems exist in the sciences and social sciences.) There are many approaches to material, many ways of interpreting it, that represent basic philosophical orientations. Two referees, sent the same manuscript, may differ as widely as one saying it is junk and should be utterly rejected, and the other saying it is brilliant and should be published as soon as possible. The editor is responsible for finding the kinds of referees who would be fair for the journal in question. If the journal has a particular orientation, one can expect the referees to judge accordingly. I am not, therefore, saying that there should be "objective" referees. I think in the nature of the case that this is not possible. But the editor should find responsible referees, ones who will give serious reasons for their judgments; who will give useful advice to the author; and, one hopes, who will do this in a fair amount of time. (My own experience is that some people will put the manuscript at the bottom of the huge pile on their desk and will find it after much prodding a half year or year later. The author by this time is frantic, since the pace of the scholarly communication process has become too leisurely, which can, of course, be deadly to people's careers).

At this point in the process, I probably take issue with a lot of present editors. Many of them see themselves as minimal arbitrators, with the referees doing the main job of deciding if something is publishable. How much should editors edit? There is an initial problem in that editors cannot be expected to know all about a field like the history of philosophy which covers over two and a half millenia, and material in many languages and fields of philosophy. Since I do not know Greek, I have to rely on people who do to judge articles involving interpretation of Greek texts. But should I just accept the referees' judgments?

When I started my career right after World War II, a former professor of mine, Paul Weiss, founded the now very well-established journal, *Review of Metaphysics*. While he edited it, he personally judged all of the articles and took on all the editorial chores. He told me he edited one issue at a time; that is, he kept no backlog, but made up his issues out of solicited and unsolicited material that came within a certain time frame. One of my first major articles began as a talk I gave to the Humanities Society of the University of Iowa. I sent it to Professor Weiss. The paper was quite large. He read it and wrote me that he would publish it if I would document everything in it. It appeared in three installments with more than two hundred footnotes. The article itself took issue with almost all of the interpreters of modern philosophy. Weiss, though I suspect he did not know all of the material I was discussing, decided on his own that my interpretation should be communicated to the scholarly world. I have reason to believe that, had he sent my article to referees, they would have told him that it should not be published because I disagreed with what was in the textbooks. This is exactly what happened when the article was expanded into a now very successful book: publishers sent it to referees, who told them that I disagreed with the accepted authorities.

Editors should edit rather than just keep score of what the referees have to say. Editors can do this by choosing referees whose negative or positive proclivities are known in advance. At present many editors of journals, book series, and the like just send out the material, receive the referee reports, and, if there is anything negative, decide to reject it without themselves looking at the material. One can say that this is bound to be the case because the amount of unsolicited submissions far exceeds what one editor, with the most good will in the world, can really read, and read carefully. (I once met Professor Weiss's successor as editor of the *Review of Metaphysics*. He told me he read everything that came in and carefully evaluated it. He did a great service for the journal, and probably for the authors, but, needless to say, he did not get tenure, because he had no time to publish on his own.) If the editor is also a teacher and an active scholar, he or she will be torn between editing in a serious sense and fulfilling the normal academic commitments. Some institutions give consideration to this and relieve editors from some duties, but most do not. A few journals, like the *American Historical Review*, make the editors full-time employees for a number of years, with no other duties. But most journals are edited on campuses by professors immersed in all that is involved in college and university life. This is probably for the best, since it keeps scholarly communication within the context of scholarly activity. But it does pose serious commitment problems for editors.

The editorial process usually involves further rewriting and reworking of the submissions, from small editorial matters about grammar, and small scholarly matters about a footnote or two, to drastic redoing of articles. This process can consume months and even years before the editor and the author agree on the content of the piece to be published. Hence the length of time between germination and acceptance can run into many years. (Scientists are complaining that the process in their fields takes six months or a year.) Then, after that, the technical process of actual publication can take two years or more. The *Journal of the History of Philosophy* has just such a backlog. Glitches in the publication process can add still more time. All too many humanistic journals run months or years behind their publication schedule for technical, financial, and distribution reasons.

I have referred to the scholarly communication process in the humanities as slow and leisurely. We do not have the scientists' problem of having to communicate immediately. (And I am not sure they have such a problem either. It would seem that we could wait a decade or a century to find out what the surface of Venus is like, since we have already waited so long. The episode about cold fusion, with the immense stakes at issue, is hardly likely in the humanities. Leibniz and Newton quarreled about who first invented the calculus, but *both* of them left most of their life's works unpublished, and only now is much of it being printed for the first time.) Questions of priority are not so important in the humanities. Influential formulations and interpretations are more important. Findings of facts can be matters on which priority is significant, especially to the author if she or he has spent lots of time in difficult archival research in antiquated libraries. Discovering a hitherto unknown work of a major author can be such a finding, where the claim to be the first to make this text known can be significant. Sometimes, in such cases, the leisurely process can be accelerated.

But the time between having a "great idea" and the scholarly world's knowing about it can be large indeed. Sometimes it is the author's fault. Wittgenstein and Heidegger, probably the two most important philosophers of the last fifty years, both procrastinated about publication. Both were highly idiosyncratic individuals. Most of the work of Wittgenstein that is now studied was published only after he died. Heidegger's major works after *Sein und Zeit* appeared long after they were written, partly because of the Hitler period. Some of our heroes like Spinoza, Hume, Hegel and Nietzsche for various reasons did not publish major works while they were alive.

Once published, a scholarly communication may not actually communicate for months or years. The fact that libraries have put the journals out on shelves, and that subscribers, usually few in number, have received their copies, is no guarantee that communication is taking place. Recently I heard from a professor about a paper I published in 1971. He had just read it and was excited about it and the topic. The same thing keeps happening to me, that I come across a paper decades and sometimes centuries old which is important to my research. Present indexes are not adequate to reveal all of these. As an example of this slow and leisurely process, I published a paper in 1950 offering a new interpretation of David Hume's skeptical philosophy. This interpretation has been accepted by many Hume scholars. In 1989 a purported refutation of my original article, and the more recent work of other Hume scholars, appeared. The author of this purported refutation had been showing it to people for several years. It is mentioned in a book published five years ago. The journal that published his refutation (namely my journal) spent several years of editorial evaluation before accepting it for publication. A well-known Hume scholar and I have agreed to write an answer, but we have not even begun, and it will be some years before our answer, if accepted, appears.

It may well be that there is nothing in philosophy that needs to be published quickly. Nothing we could figure out is like cold fusion. We are supposed to be looking for The Truth and the Good Life. The discussion of such issues can go on informally regardless of the slow, leisurely pace of formal communication. This can happen through correspondence, lectures, and discussions. The formal communication could be speeded up if there were more man- and woman-power and more financial resources. (We operate on a mere pittance compared to scientific journals.) But whether this is desirable is debatable. The pace could be improved with more money expended and greater subscription costs. But with the present financial crunch at almost all libraries, this would most probably be counter-productive.

Because new perspectives, outlooks, and methods are being put forward, new journals are continually being created to present new ideas and points of view. Letting new voices be heard and new topics explored is an important aspect of the communication process. The present financial difficulties of journals and libraries will have a baleful effect on this. The appropriation of journals by large publishing conglomerates, which raise the subscription costs inordinately and often decrease the size of the journal, will curtail the possibilities for new journals as well as older ones with few subscribers.

In conclusion, I think that scholars in the humanities are in a sad period as concerns formal communication because of economic trends beyond our control. However, I would hope that, by-and-large, we can continue the slow, leisurely, present process, because experience over the centuries indicates the need for more time for consideration and gestation of ideas. Various technical developments can cut down some of the time involved. But I do not think we should try to emulate our scientific colleagues. I recently read in a scientific publication that 95 percent of what is presently known about brain chemistry was published in the last ten years. This indicates that most scientific publication becomes obsolete very soon and has a half-life of 5 to 10 years at most. In the humanities we are still studying what was written decades and centuries ago. We are carrying on a discussion with a long tradition of intellectual ancestors. The process by which we do it may inhibit quick discussion with our contemporaries except by informal means. But, perhaps it is the best that we can devise at the present time. (And, as a closing comment, since no one is likely to put up the resources that would be needed to accelerate our communication, we may as well make a virtue of the way we do it.)

Scientific Publication: Science News

Daniel B. Menzel

SUMMARY. Scientific advances are occurring at such a rapid pace that scientific communications are becoming more like print news media. Scientists want rapid publication and electronic retrieval, but, at the same time, demand careful peer review and criticism of their work. Conventional journals, in which a year or more may ensue between writing and publishing, are ill-equipped to meet these demands. Electronic typesetting and rapid distribution systems of modern publishers are not the slow step in the process; getting rapid competent review is now the critical factor. Scientific publication will lead the way in publication in non-print media and in electronic transfer of reviews. The "electronic book" is closer to reality in primary literature than anywhere else in scientific publication.

PAPER WAS UNAVAILABLE AT TIME OF PUBLICATION

Daniel B. Menzel is Professor and Chairman, Department of Community and Environmental Medicine, University of California, Irvine, CA 92713. He is also Managing Editor of *Toxicology Letters*.

Publish *and* Perish

Alain L. Hénon

Here is the scenario: An industry noted for its very large product line and for its well-defined and limited market discovers that this market is shrinking rapidly due to a shift in the allocation of funds to the purchase of other products that are not now produced by the industry, and to the disappearance of a number of customers from the market. At the same time, competition is increasing from new entries into the industry. The number of units sold of each of its products is often reduced by half or more over a period of ten years. What should the industry do to reverse the pattern? Two obvious solutions come to mind: (1) reduce the number of products offered and concentrate on those that have the best sale; and (2) find out what its customers are now buying and add it to the line.

Instead, the industry has done the unexpected: it has increased the variety of products offered, further depressing the average number of units sold of each product offered. And it has resolutely continued the traditional product line, generally rejecting any attempt at modifying it to fit more closely the desires and needs of its customers.

We call that industry scholarly publishing. University presses, the world in which I work, are an even more peculiar subset of that industry.

University presses were founded in order to provide an outlet for early victims of the publish or perish syndrome. Universities discovered that commercial publishers were unwilling to publish the specialized work of their faculties, and so they took matters into their own hands. They founded what in effect were university van-

Alain L. Hénon is Assistant Director, Serials Publications, University of California Press, 2120 Berkeley Way, Berkeley, CA 94720.

ity presses, providing funds to publish material for which most publishers depending on the bottom line knew there was no market. As it turned out, those publishers were wrong: they failed to realize that the same people who founded the university presses also purchased the resulting products for their academic libraries. So a fairly neat, very incestuous system evolved: institutions of higher learning paid to have the work of their faculty published, and then made sure their libraries had the funds to purchase the resulting books and journals. When I joined the university press world in 1966, the University of California Press still benefited from almost 500 standing orders from libraries which would purchase everything that carried our imprint, sight unseen. And one could count on at least another 500 library orders for most monographs. We now count ourselves lucky to have 100 standing orders and total institutional sales of 400. Obviously the market has changed. And what have we and other university presses done in response? We have printed fewer copies, which has driven the unit cost up; which has driven the price up; which has lowered the sales further.

In short, university presses have traditionally not been market-driven organizations. University press people have been heard proudly to proclaim that the market is irrelevant to their enterprise: what they are really about is publishing "great scholarship," and the libraries are foolish if they do not beat a path to their door. Fortunately or unfortunately, depending on your point of view, there is a great deal of truth to the statement. Although one hears a lot of rhetoric from university press marketing managers, the presses still exist mainly to publish specialized scholarship. A glance at a university press seasonal catalog shows very little change in the type of title listed over the past forty years. Once one is past the first few pages in which press editors and marketeers try to convince book stores that they really are trade publishers by listing such unconventional university press items as cookbooks, the type becomes smaller and the titles become longer. Comparing the Fall 1950 catalog and the Fall 1988 catalog of the University of California Press is an interesting exercise. Can anyone guess in which of the two catalogs the following titles were published:

— *A Self-Governing Dominion: California, 1849-1860*;
— *The Dusky-Footed Wood Rat* (with the wonderful first sentence of the catalog description: "This study of wood rats is mainly concerned with the affairs of individual rodents . . .");
— *Dioscorus of Aphrodito: His Work and His World*;
— *Phylogenetic Relationships Among Advanced Snakes*?

There has been a definite change, however: in 1989 the University of California Press is publishing over 40 percent more monographs than it did in 1950. Similar figures can be cited for most university presses as well as for those commercial publishers who found out money could be made by publishing scholarship. And all this is occurring in the face of a shrinking market.

A recent book I handled was published after receiving glowing reports from academic reviewers, and then was very well received in all the right academic journals. It sold 308 copies, worldwide! It would have been demonstrably cheaper for everyone concerned for the author to go to the local copy shop and have 400 copies made and shipped to every major library in the world. The book I am talking about cost the University of California Press around $35,000 to produce, including overhead costs. To date, the book has brought in a little over $10,000 in income, leaving the Press with a deficit of around $25,000. To copy 624 manuscript pages (the original form of the book), and to bind and ship the result to 400 libraries costs a bit less than $10,000; except, of course, that it would not have qualified as a "publication" on the author's curriculum vitae, and libraries hardly welcome such unsolicited "gifts." Clearly, university presses perform a service in reviewing, selecting, editing, and producing such manuscripts in some sort of acceptable format. The question remains, however, whether such effort and expense is not simply wasted when only 300 customers can be found for the end product.

If one asks the author of such books if the effort was wasted, the answer is obvious: of course not! Most academic authors receive rewards for publishing that are not dependent upon the number of copies actually sold. A large percentage of the books and journal articles published each year by university presses (and now some commercial presses) are not written with ANY market in mind, and the ultimate number of customers or their wishes are quite irrelevant. The purpose at hand is to get something in print with a respectable publisher so that the academic promotional system can continue to operate. The driving force behind the increase in the number of books and journals, and also behind the increase in size of many journals, is the need for an increased number of academics to publish, and, at least in some disciplines where competition is particularly fierce, to publish more. And by "publish" it is meant that manuscripts will be reviewed according to some quite specific procedures, by a publisher generally well thought of in an academic discipline. University presses thus become the essential vehicles through which academics receive advancement. The academic community as a whole has little concern about any ultimate customer (let alone a reader!) willing to pay the ever-increasing price for the result. Very few academics are aware that there may be some problem in the distribution of scholarly information. Authors often will say to a press that their book or journal will sell to "all academic libraries." They are generally shocked at the response I give: there are fewer than 200 major research libraries in the United States, and can anyone expect many other libraries to purchase a book on Dioscorus of Aphrodito's life and times?

There are indications that something is going to happen to change all this. A number of people are calling for fundamental change in scholarly communication, of which the tenure system and its publish or perish imperative is a major factor. I am impressed by the fact that librarians seem to be preparing for that change and taking an active role in it. I am afraid that a number of publishers, especially university presses, are going to be found lacking in any real plans to face that change. I say this because I have noticed how badly university presses have dealt with the technological revolution that is at hand, a technological revolution that may provide the solution to the dilemma facing them.

Richard Lanham, who makes it part of his business as an English professor to look at what he calls the "Digital Revolution," recently began an article with the following challenging statement: "Perhaps the real question for literary study now is not whether our students will be reading Great Traditional Books or Relevant Modern ones in the future, but whether they will be reading books at all." He goes on to say that literary scholars must adapt to and adopt the new technology less they find themselves "making the pianos while someone else makes the music."[1]

I think I may be working for a piano maker in an age where electronic keyboards are all the rage. We have barely entered the electronic age in scholarly publishing. In fact, our authors are often much more familiar with computers and word-processors than most of our employees are. I do not know of anyone in scholarly publishing with the kind of insight and understanding of this new world of electronic "publishing" demonstrated by Professor Lanham. Our institutional customers are far ahead of us in the application of modern technology to the distribution and storage of information.

University presses are still deeply committed to the idea that the act of publishing implies that the end product will be in the form of a collection of sheets of paper, bound together, and sold as a unit. A few, far seeing individuals within the industry have realized that "publishing" might mean issuing a recording, a film, a videotape, or perhaps even a hypercard stack; but as a whole these are seen as experiments, and whenever one fails, as inevitably many do, they are gleefully pointed to as one more indication that "books are here to stay."

I would modify that statement to say "some books are here to stay." It is still impossible to imagine something quite as convenient as the mass market paperback. Its contents can be "accessed" anywhere, at any time, in any order, and the paper on which it is printed can even find secondary usage (I have lit many a camp fire with the first chapter of some cheap novel!).

But one does not read about advanced snakes on the beach. In fact, it may be fairly said that one does not read such books at all, if by "reading" one means proceeding from page one to page 359 in a strictly linear manner. One can argue that most monographs are "consulted," insofar as the user looks in the index for items of interest, and then reads that chapter or portion of chapter that is cited. (Hence, incidentally, the increasing importance of good indexes.) The same is true for journals: the user looks at the table of contents and then turns to that portion of the issue that is of interest, often to copy it for future use, while discarding the balance of the issue. It is an extremely wasteful system, and any number of electronic solutions to the problem spring to mind. None so far has imposed itself, partly because technology is moving so rapidly; but, sooner or later, something that everyone can accept and afford will present itself—probably sooner.

What is going to happen? First, I believe that within the next few years the crisis in the publication of monographic works of scholarship will deepen: the number of libraries willing and able to purchase even a moderate percentage of all the titles published is going to be so small as to make publication impossible even with massive subsidies. This will be especially true in the humanities and social sciences, where publishing a book is still considered an essential step for gaining respect among one's colleagues. In the hard sciences, the crisis will be focussed on journals; even without any profiteering by some publishers, the price of journals will continue to escalate as the number of pages published increases in response to authors' demand for more outlets for their work. At some point, and we are very close to it today, libraries are going to have to act in ways that may make it impossible economically for some publishers to continue issuing journals.

Second, the crisis will force scholarly publishers to become more aware of their market and less responsive to their authors. An index of this is the fact that I am here, speaking to a group made up in large numbers by librarians, rather than knocking on doors in some academic institution looking for manuscripts.

This market sensitivity in turn will force a revision of the publish or perish ideal on the academic community, and it is quite likely that scholarly publishers will no longer act in their traditional manner as guarantors of the quality of work produced by individual scholars. What will replace it is anybody's guess; but it is clear that the current reviewing process, whereby scholars are judged mainly by their output of printed material published by so-called "respectable" outlets, is too expensive. Some university presses may lose their very reason for being. (Unless, of course, they are maintained by university administrations as useful public relations institutions; there are signs that some universities already look upon their presses in that way.) Others will find ways of redefining their role in the academic community.

Richard Dougherty, in a recent issue of *The Chronicle of Higher Education*, calls for precisely this kind of redefinition.[2] In particular, he calls for the marriage of university presses, computer centers, and libraries to publish scientific and scholarly publications. Libraries certainly have come a long way toward being distributors (also known as "publishers") of information, as opposed to simply storage places for scholarly material. The first copying machine made available to the general public in a library made that institution a publisher, specifically, a reprint publisher. Libraries, it seems to me, are threatening to replace university presses as the principal agents for the distribution of scholarly information. I think they are doing this rather reluctantly and would welcome increased participation by university presses in solving the crisis at hand. Some of us have entered into a dialogue, from which we may eventually come out as friends rather than enemies. Speaking as one university press publisher, I believe it is imperative that we tackle this problem together.

NOTES

1. See Richard A. Lanham, "The Electronic Word: Literary Study and the Digital Revolution," *New Literary History* 20 (1988-89): 265-290.
2. Richard M. Dougherty, "To Meet the Crisis in Journal Costs, Universities Must Reassert Their Role in Scholarly Publishing," *The Chronicle of Higher Education*, April 12, 1989.

Scholarly Communication and the Role of Libraries: Problems and Possibilities for Accessing Journal Articles

David J. Cohen

In a sense, it seems mistaken to suggest that there is any problem with the process of scholarly communication. These days scholars are communicating at staggering rates. An article in the *Journal of Social Behavior and Personality* notes that professors in the sciences alone generate articles for 40,000 journals at the rate of two articles per minute each day—well over 1,000,000 articles per year.[1] Scholarly communication is not in jeopardy, but the organization, delivery, and control of that burgeoning literature may well be.

Ironically, libraries, which we all readily recognize as the institutions that bear the stewardship responsibility for information, have only a limited (and perhaps diminishing) role for organizing, controlling, and delivering information among scholars. The American Council of Learned Societies recently surveyed humanists and social scientists for their views on libraries and computers, as well as the research and publication process. Their major findings are troubling. Most scholars indicated that they are not able to keep up with the literature in their fields. Moreover, they do not rate libraries high on the list of resources required for their research, and they are not using the new technologies that libraries offer for accessing information.[2] Another recent study of faculty in the social sciences at

---

David J. Cohen is Director of Libraries, Robert Scott Small Library, College of Charleston, Charleston, SC 29424.

the University of Wisconsin revealed even less reliance on libraries. When asked to rank eighteen sources of information, faculty "rated private collections as more important than every source of information directly related to the library, ranking only journals and tracking citations as more important."[3]

The survey literature on scholarly communication only confirms what many librarians observe daily. When was the last time you saw a faculty member at the index tables? I doubt if anyone in this room believes that a majority of scholars use the resources of the library efficiently or effectively. Some significant portion do not even frequent the place. They may send a graduate student occasionally to retrieve a known item or perhaps request an interlibrary loan. Those scholars who do use libraries follow time-honored practices. Often they have an article in hand. Usually they received it informally from a colleague, not via the library. The article has footnotes and they search for the citations. Others simply come to the library and browse through favored journals.

The evidence thus indicates that scholars make poor use of their libraries. Why? I am really not sure. In the remainder of this presentation I am going to suggest that there are some problems with journal indexing. I am also going to recommend some improvements. Still, I am uneasy suggesting remedies because we know so very little about how scholars work. If we are going to expand the role of libraries in scholarly communication, we need to learn more about the process of doing research.

Journals have been called the currency of scholarly communication. Ostensibly, indexes and abstracts offer control of the scholarly literature (which scholars complain that they are unable to keep up with anyway). Yet printed indexes and abstracts have failed to provide effective links in the process of scholarly communication because, I suggest, scholars find looking for information in them a chaotic, exasperating, and bewildering experience.[4] Contrast the index with the card catalog or even the online catalog. Indexes present an endless variety of nonstandard approaches for retrieving citations to scholarly journals. Some use controlled subject headings but the authorities differ. Some use a keyword approach. Some have separate author and subject indexes. Others combine authors and subjects in a dictionary approach. Almost all indexes and abstracts display the citations differently. Even when a search for a journal article can be limited to one index, the citations are rarely cumulated; most often, faculty face a series of annual volumes which must be individually searched. When cumulations exist, they do not reflect the complete run of a journal. Printed indexes have another limitation: the coverage is not current because it takes time to produce an index in printed form.

There are other problems with printed indexes. Unlike the card catalog, printed indexes attempt to provide all of the citations on a given topic whether or not the library owns the cited journals. While some faculty require this degree of comprehensiveness, many others are simply frustrated by it. Nothing aggravates researchers more than retrieving an article citation which seems right on target only to find that the library does not own the journal.

Recently, some library professionals have begun to change the systems for locating information in scholarly journals. Escalating costs for library materials and developments in technology have led libraries to introduce computerized systems for searching and retrieving bibliographic citations to journal articles. At present, there are at least three evolving models which provide scholars with the means to locate journal articles. These approaches are:

- online reference database searching using BRS, DIALOG or similar gateways;
- licensing and mounting journal article citation databases on local computer systems; and,
- CD-ROM systems.

While these models each have certain advantages, they also replicate many of the undesirable features of printed indexes. The separation of journal citation files from book information files (i.e., card or online catalogs) remains, since none of the applications integrate both types into one system. Moreover, journal article citations are still splintered into a variety of separate and distinct files. Like most libraries, ours offers access to over three hundred indexes via BRS and DIALOG—far more than we own in print format. Online searching via BRS or DIALOG CD-ROM indexes must be supplemented by printed indexes for comprehensive searches. Librarians usually mediate the search process in the automated environment because it requires skills and expertise that many faculty do not have. By directing them to the "appropriate" index, librarians make decisions which categorize inquiries and limit the responses. Furthermore, while many users can search printed indexes simultaneously, CD-ROM and online searching limit users to a fixed number of workstations. Many libraries resort to signup schedules for people who use these systems.

The dissimilarities between the various CD-ROM indexes confuse faculty and students. Familiar with the general subject approach of the online catalog for books, they do not recognize the very specific subject focus of the CD-ROMs. (I recently found a music historian searching ABI/INFORM for something about Handel!) Although work on standardization continues, as it has for years with printed indexes, few computerized indexes use standard search methodologies or displays. The MLA on CD-ROM has different search conventions from ERIC on CD-ROM. Yet a scholar must search both if he or she is preparing a study on English pedagogy. Citation displays present particular problems since the same journal titles are abbreviated differently in different indexes.

Still, I do not want to belittle the advantages of computerization. Rather, I would like to propose a new approach, namely, merging machine readable journal article citations with other bibliographic records already found in the online catalog. This approach vastly simplifies location routines for all library users. The online catalog I propose would have the following features:

- journal article citations from the library's most highly used journals;
- citations for books, journal articles, journal titles, films, videotapes, material in any format, retrieved and displayed together in the online catalog;
- journal article citation records stored in a quasi-MARC format;
- identical "search engines" for searching journal article citations as well as other types of citations in the online catalog;
- keyword access with Boolean operators; and,
- authority-controlled access for authors and subjects.

At the College of Charleston we are in the very preliminary

stages of planning for the addition of journal article citations to our online catalog. I would like to share some of our ideas with you.

At this time the library collection includes approximately 3,400 periodical and other serial titles. While it may not be possible to have a machine readable record for every article the library owns, it is feasible to obtain a record for nearly 1,000 journal titles. H. W. Wilson, for example, can provide tape subscriptions for the journals which it indexes. The library will add records from the last five years, renewing the database periodically through tape subscription updates and dropping coverage of journals more than five years old. Moreover, the library will only add citations for articles from the journals it owns. Library users will still have to consult indexes and abstracts for older citations and for citations to journals we do not own. This approach mirrors the bibliographic organization and control for monographs.

Although the data tapes available from a vendor like H. W. Wilson are comprised of journal article citations, they are not currently organized into a standard format. In order to introduce them into the library's online catalog, we will need to modify the citations for journal articles. Fortunately, it is possible to undertake the programming which will translate and tag the records in a quasi-MARC format. The College of Charleston plans to contract with Data Research Associates for programming to display the journal citations, especially the holdings data, according to the appropriate standards in the online catalog. At the same time, the Catalog Department may be responsible for enriching some of the data by introducing subject authorities. The result will be bibliographic records for journal articles which can be searched in the library computer system, Atlas, in all of the ways people now search our online catalog.

This approach is quite different from that of the evolving models. When library users look for journal article citations in indexes and abstracts, even on CD-ROM, they must learn a series of different search methods. The conventions for searching *Chemical Abstracts* differ from *Humanities Index*. None of the indexes or abstracts uses the search methodology of the online catalog, but merging the journal article citations with those for books will simplify retrieval. While this approach is particularly appropriate in an undergraduate institution, even the most sophisticated researchers will benefit from a standard approach to searching. One key element in this approach is the experimental use of the name and subject authorities from the Library of Congress. While keyword searching offers many avenues for access to the journal article citations, the use of controlled vocabulary subject headings will avoid the potentially chaotic overload of irrelevant citations that keyword searching can produce.

Simply put, at the College of Charleston we believe that introducing machine readable records, organized according to accepted standards for citations of journal articles, and including only citations from journals owned by the library, will increase the use of the library's journal collections more than any other existing model.

Pressed by researchers, libraries have invested heavily in journal collections. Conversely, they have made minimal investment in access and control systems for journals. Compare your costs for indexes, abstracts, and serials cataloging with your costs for organizing book collections. The latter include all cataloging costs, all costs paid to the bibliographic utility, and most costs of local automated systems (since a primary function of local systems is replication of card catalogs). Clearly, libraries spend far more money organizing and cataloging books than they do serials, but this must change. If libraries are to play a vital role in scholarly communication, they need to reflect their investment in journals. Technology will facilitate better systems for locating citations to journal articles. How libraries apply the technology will determine how successful they will be in sustaining and expanding their role in the scholarly communication process.

NOTES

1. Cited in Charles J. Sykes, *ProfScam: Professors and the Demise of Higher Education* (Washington: Regnery Gateway, 1988), 115.
2. Ronald H. Epp and Joan S. Segal, "The ACLS Survey and Academic Library Service," *College and Research Libraries News* 48 (February, 1987): 67-8.
3. Mary B. Folster, "A Study of the Use of Information Sources by Social Science Researchers," *The Journal of Academic Librarianship* 15 (March, 1989): 7-11.
4. Some of the ideas in this section will appear shortly in a forthcoming article by the author in *The Journal of Academic Librarianship*.

CD-ROM IN LIBRARIES: REVOLUTION OR REVOLT?

CD-ROM in Libraries: Access, Trends and Challenges

Karen Sandlin Silverman

I am pleased to be here to start off today's presentations with a discussion of the impact that CD-ROM technology has had on libraries. Since many CD-ROM products are, by nature, serial publications, this is a timely topic for us to tackle here at NASIG. I have been joined today by Beth Juhl from Columbia University and by Joe Michalak from SilverPlatter. I will try to lay a framework for our discussion by introducing the topic. Joe will share with us his view of CD-ROM technology in libraries from his perspective as a vendor. Beth will detail Columbia's experiences in adopting this new technology. We plan to allow approximately 45 minutes for reactions and discussion among the panelists and the audience. Please hold your questions until the end of the formal presentations.

As I mentioned, CD-ROM products are typically serial publications. For example, of the 29 databases listed in the Winter 1989

Formerly Assistant Manager of PALINET's OCLC Services Group, Karen Sandlin Silverman is now Information Services Manager, Robert Morris Associates, 1 Liberty Place, 1650 Market Street, Suite 2300, Philadelphia, PA 19103.

© 1990 by The Haworth Press, Inc. All rights reserved.

SilverPlatter catalog, 23, or approximately 75 percent, are available only on a subscription basis. CD-ROM subscriptions usually run for a one-year period and involve quarterly updates. Of the seven SilverPlatter databases available for purchase, only one is available only by out-and-out purchase. Two databases have the purchase option available only for archival discs, and four databases are available either through subscription or purchase. Clearly we are talking of serial publications.

Before I relay specific information to you regarding the topic at hand, I would like to provide some background on what PALINET has been doing with CD-ROM.

For over one-half century, PALINET, or the Pennsylvania Area Library Network, has been a leader in providing bibliographic services to the library community. Its membership of over 300 libraries and information centers represents all types and sizes of institutions located in Delaware, Maryland, New Jersey, Pennsylvania, and the District of Columbia. As you can see from Figure 1, our membership includes all types of libraries. The majority of our membership, 54 percent, is academic libraries.

PALINET grew out of the Union Library Catalogue of Pennsylvania, which was founded as a W.P.A. Project in the mid-1930s. PALINET was reorganized in 1975 as a broker of computer-based services to libraries with a mission to assist member libraries in their automation efforts. Operating as a not-for-profit multi-type library cooperative, PALINET is a diversified network engaged in developing, producing, marketing, and supporting computer-based products and services to its members.

Over the past decade PALINET's primary focus has been the support and brokering of OCLC services, essentially adding value to OCLC products in return for an annual membership fee. PALINET is one of approximately 20 library networks delivering OCLC services at the state or regional level.

In addition to OCLC services, PALINET brokers and supports a variety of automated library services. Included among these services are: on-going continuing education programs and workshops on topics related to library automation; brokering of online databases offered through BRS, DIALOG, VU/TEXT, and WILSONLINE; and magnetic tape processing services to help li-

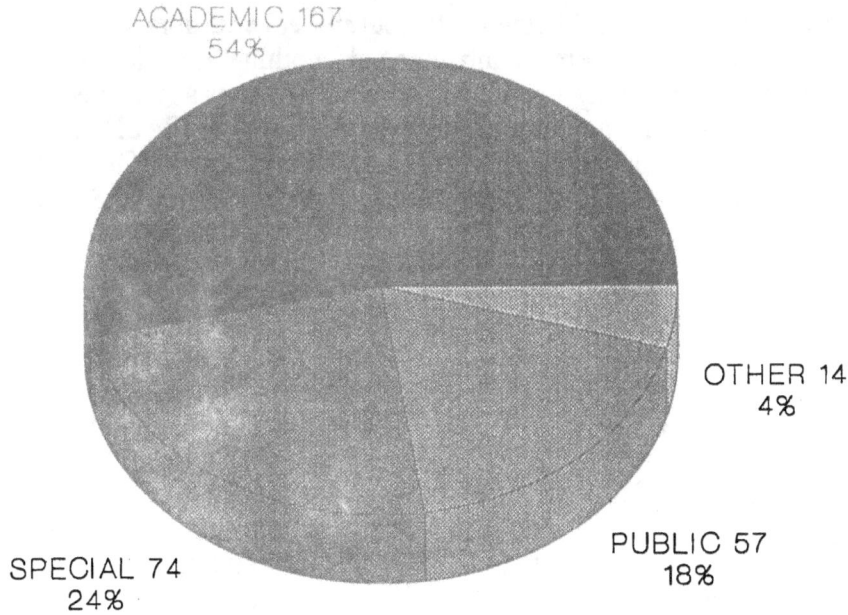

FIGURE 1. PALINET Membership by Type, May 1989.
(Total: 312)

braries prepare MARC records for loading into local systems and group databases.

In 1984 OCLC introduced its first microcomputer-based workstation, the M300. This development, combined with the growth of the microcomputer industry, led PALINET to launch a new service program in July 1984. Through the Microcomputer Support Services Program, or MSSP, PALINET members can obtain advice on hardware and software purchasing decisions, learn various software packages, and even order software and hardware at reduced costs. PALINET has a microcomputer training laboratory that can comfortably hold 12 people for hands-on training sessions. These courses cover a wide range of topics from Introduction to Microcomputers, or Introduction to DOS, to Desktop Publishing and Hypertext. Training is available for a number of popular software packages, including WordPerfect, Lotus 1-2-3, and dBASE IV.

PALINET staff have always taken great pride in staying on top of new technologies and being on the cutting edge in library automation. Indeed, the membership demands nothing less. Many PALINET members wish to embrace new technologies as they become available, and the membership has grown to rely on PALINET for assistance. To that end, PALINET jumped on the CD-ROM bandwagon two years ago with the founding of the CD-ACCESS program.

PALINET'S CD-ACCESS PROGRAM

CD-ACCESS is a program to help member libraries implement and use CD-ROM products. The program currently consists of four main components.

First, PALINET staff offer assistance in making decisions regarding hardware purchases and software subscriptions. Staff monitor hardware compatibility problems and solutions and keep track of the features of the various CD-ROM drives in the market.

Second, PALINET staff conduct a number of different workshops pertaining to CD-ROM technology in libraries. These workshops run the gamut from introductory overview workshops to hands-on training on particular products.

Third, PALINET procures hardware for member libraries at discounted prices. This can involve merely a CD-ROM drive or it could be an order for a half dozen complete workstations.

Last, PALINET has contracts with nine CD-ROM database vendors to provide subscriptions to members at a discounted rate. In addition to the discounted price, the program offers the convenience of allowing libraries to use funds that may already be on deposit in their PALINET cash accounts and of adding CD-ROM products to already established PALINET accounting services.

PALINET brokers CD-ROM products from the following vendors:

- R. R. Bowker products, including *Books in Print Plus* and *Ulrich's Plus*.
- Online Research Systems CD-Plus products, including MEDLINE.
- DIALOG products, including ERIC and MEDLINE.

- the *Facts on File News Digest*
- the Microsoft Bookshelf.
- OCLC Search CD450 products, including the ICP Software Information Database, AGRICOLA, ERIC, NTIS, and *Selected Water Resources Abstracts*. OCLC also offers a number of databases derived from its Online Union Catalog including the Education Library.
- PAIS, the *Public Affairs Information Service*.
- SilverPlatter products including ERIC, CINAHL (Nursing and Allied Health), MEDLINE, and *PsycLIT*.
- H. W. Wilson products, including *Readers Guide to Periodical Literature, Social Sciences Index, Humanities Index*, and *Business Periodicals Index*.

A new area which PALINET is exploring is the support and possible brokering of local area networks for CD-ROM applications.

Although the CD-ACCESS program has only been in existence for two years, it has been a rousing success. Over one third of PALINET's member libraries have purchased hardware and/or subscribed to software through the program. Many more of our libraries have simply attended workshops and received information from us. PALINET has survived the first round of renewal processing for many libraries, and some of the earliest innovators have even begun processing their second year renewals for CD-ROM subscriptions.

Because of the success of the program and PALINET's relative maturity in dealing with CD-ROM technologies, I believe that PALINET's experiences with CD-ROM implementation and use in libraries should provide a useful picture of the niche that CD-ROM technology is carving out in libraries.

Figure 2 illustrates the popularity of various CD-ROM products in PALINET member libraries. SilverPlatter and Wilson products have proven most popular in these libraries, but the other vendors are holding their own. Currently 45 PALINET libraries subscribe to 103 SilverPlatter databases, and 36 PALINET libraries subscribe to 106 Wilson databases. Figure 3 shows a breakdown of CD-ROM activity by type of library. PALINET's academic libraries have

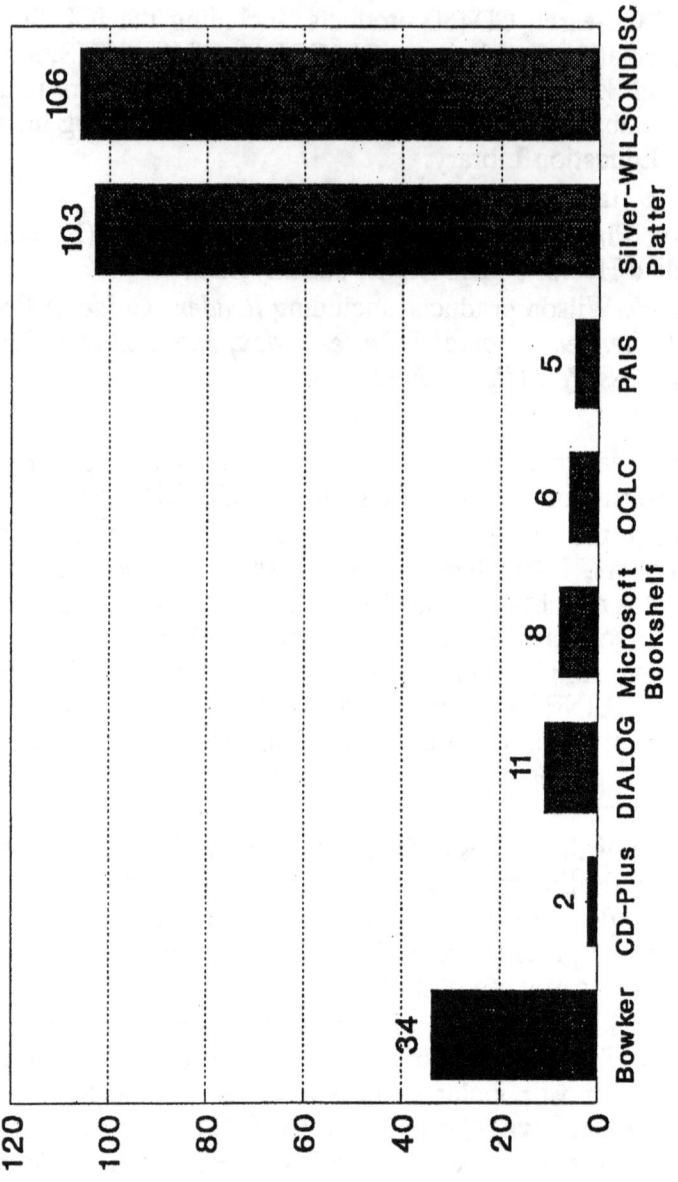

FIGURE 2. CD-ROM Subscriptions by Vendor

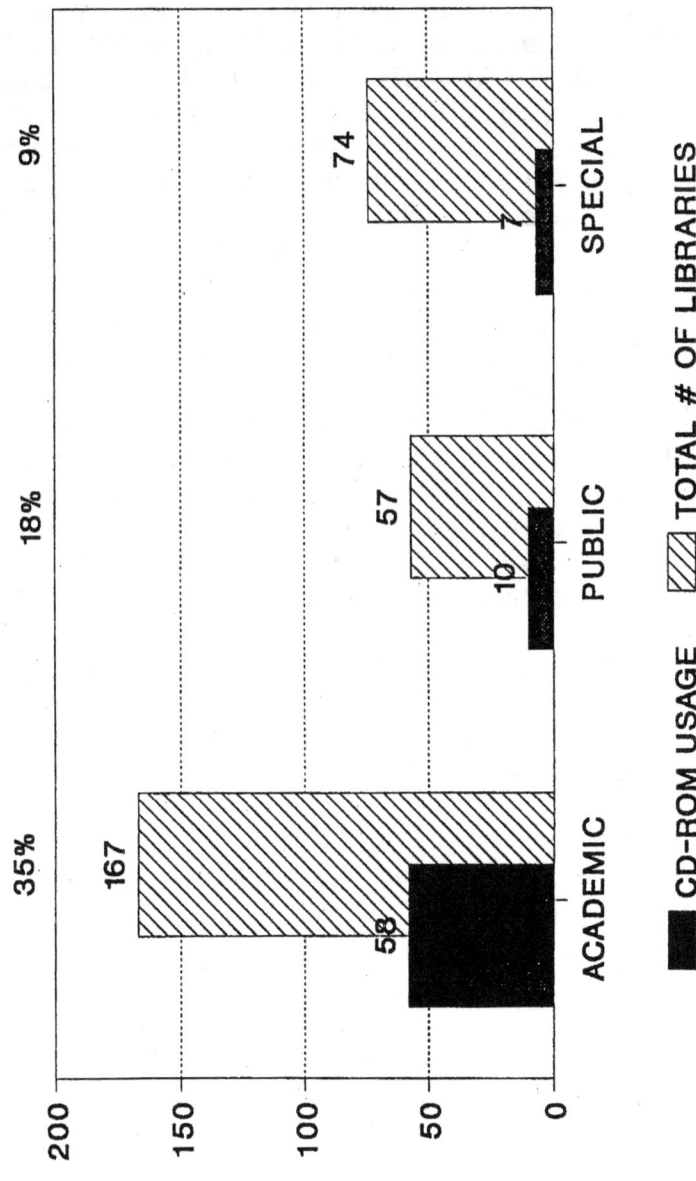

FIGURE 3. CD-ROM Subscriptions by Library Type

shown the most interest in CD-ROM to date (35 percent), but public and special libraries are also exploring the technology.

My statistics represent only some of the CD-ROM activity taking place in PALINET libraries. Not all PALINET libraries obtain CD-ROM products through PALINET. In the state of Pennsylvania, many libraries participate in the ACCESS Pennsylvania project, whereby the holdings of many Pennsylvania libraries have been mastered onto a CD-ROM union catalog by the Brodart Company. These catalogs include bibliographic records and holdings information. They are updated annually and are distributed on two CD-ROM discs. The catalog is available free of charge to any Pennsylvania library. In the state of New Jersey, there are several regional projects currently underway to provide regional union catalogs on compact discs. The state of Maryland has contracted with Auto-Graphics to produce MicroCat, a union catalog on CD-ROM.

Some PALINET libraries have opted to master their catalogs onto CD-ROM and use these as public access catalogs. Others are exploring the use of CD-ROM catalogs as back-ups to their online public access catalogs. There are also a number of CD-ROM products not available through PALINET to which some members have subscribed.

So far, I have been talking mostly of CD-ROM reference products. There are also a number of popular technical services products available. For example, many PALINET members are now exploring implementation of OCLC's CD-ROM based cataloging product, CAT CD450.

I suspect more than a third of PALINET membership is involved with CD-ROM in some manner, but formal surveying is needed to measure this activity accurately.

TRENDS

One phenomenon I have witnessed is that librarians have become the innovators in the use of CD-ROM technology. Many of the CD-ROM products on the market have clear applications to library service programs and lend themselves well to the library setting. Some PALINET librarians report that their data processing and computer center personnel are now turning to the library for advice and information about this new technology because of the key role librarians are playing with regard to CD-ROM.

I find it interesting that CD-ROM products have achieved an incredible degree of popularity in such a short period of time in libraries. Many libraries have had to order additional workstations to accommodate overflow crowds waiting for access to CD-ROM databases. It is absolutely devastating when the inevitable hardware and/or software problems occur—how do microcomputers sense final exam time? Two PALINET libraries have opted to live with inoperable floppy disk drives until term break rather than incur the wrath of the students for sending the machines away for repairs.

When I first started working with the CD-ACCESS program I thought that all the CD-ROM vendors who are generous with their trial offer programs were being just that—extremely generous. I have since learned just how naive I was, since the majority of the trial offers in PALINET libraries have turned into sales. These vendors are not being merely generous—they recognize a good marketing strategy when they see one. It is difficult to take CD-ROM products out of the library once patrons have discovered them.

This brings us to a discussion of funding CD-ROM products. How are libraries paying for these subscriptions? Many libraries are using special funds and grant monies for the initial implementation of CD-ROM services.[1] One of PALINET's most successful libraries in this area received a grant from the Department of Higher Education in New Jersey for $90,000 to promote undergraduate education through the use of CD-ROM technology. The library purchased eight workstations and subscribed to 19 CD-ROM products through PALINET during the year of the grant. Of the initial subscriptions, four were cancelled at renewal time because of low popularity, but the library added three new databases for a net loss of only one database in the second year. Fortunately, the library was able to fund renewals without drastically cutting services in other areas. This was done by gradually shifting the serials budget to cover CD-ROM subscriptions. The library has simply made CD-ROM a priority at this time and justifies the expense to its administration through an argument based on the effectiveness of good programs.

Even though this library is committed to CD-ROM, the staff are still hesitant to cut hard copy subscriptions. This reluctance is common in libraries. Many have yet to tackle the issue of cancelling print and online counterparts to cover the expense of CD-ROM products. Most PALINET librarians are afraid to make the cuts. I am aware of only one PALINET library that has cut a print subscription in response to the acquisition of a CD-ROM database. Since this library cut a *second* copy of the print version of *Readers' Guide to Periodical Literature*, I am not sure this really counts! The most common argument made against cutting print subscriptions is that when you cancel a print subscription, you retain all items purchased. With CD-ROM products, typically, all compact discs, software, and manuals must be returned to the vendor upon cancellation. Another strong argument used against cutting print subscriptions is that print subscriptions offer the advantage of multi-user access, whereas multi-user access of CD-ROM products is an expensive proposition at this point. Online access to current information is another necessity for libraries prior to cutting print subscriptions.[2]

These factors put libraries in the position of constantly having to scrape together the money to support CD-ROM products and to look for creative ways of funding. One of our librarians reports that he is currently trying to convince various academic departments to foot the bill for databases in their subject areas. He has targeted the Education Department first and is trying to get them to pick up the tab for a subscription to ERIC on CD-ROM. He is threatening to cancel products if necessary funding does not come through. He also likes to set up as many trial offers as possible as an internal marketing strategy. He is having moderate success, and this model is being adopted by other libraries.[3]

Many libraries seem to renew all their subscriptions, even those originally funded with grant monies. As I mentioned before, once CD-ROM products are introduced in the library, patrons cannot bear the thought of living without them. This patron reaction also shows that most librarians have been wise in their selection policies, since they have chosen databases that have proven most popular. Even one member library that cancelled multiple products at renewal time did so simply in order to fund competitive products. The librarians decided they preferred the ERIC and MEDLINE products offered by another vendor.

Most PALINET libraries are still struggling with the integration of CD-ROM services into existing library service programs, but I would argue that the trend has become *acceptance* of CD-ROM services in libraries as integral parts of overall library services. I seem to receive change of address notices for subscription information almost weekly. The addresses are being changed to the serials or acquisitions departments so that at last the experts are taking over the order processing functions. CD-ROM orders are no longer special orders placed solely by the library director.

One PALINET library reports that cancellation and subscription decisions for CD-ROM databases are now being made in conjunction with the library's overall collection development program. CD-ROM databases have become simply alternative forms for core library materials—they are no longer treated like "new toys."

There has been a revival of interest in the concept of end-user searching because of the enormous popularity of CD-ROM technology in libraries. Many libraries are reexamining existing bibliographic instruction and end-user searching programs to determine the best way to fold CD-ROM technology into their programs. Some libraries are pleased to offer formalized end-user searching programs for the first time with the introduction of CD-ROM databases into their libraries. Often this process involves more than simply instructing patrons how to use a particular product, but may also be an opportunity to teach the concept of Boolean searching.

Has CD-ROM technology been revolutionary in libraries? In many ways the answer is yes. However, I think a better description of CD-ROM integration into libraries is acceptance. CD-ROM seems to be here to stay, but it does bring with it a few challenges.

CHALLENGES

CD-ROM has presented many challenges to libraries. Fortunately, librarians have shown they are up for them. Libraries have had to deal with such training issues as: training staff in the use of the CD-ROM product or products; training staff in the use of microcomputers; and training the end users. One particularly thorny training dilemma is how to teach the limitations of CD-ROM technology and the relevance of searching one database over another. It is a challenge to teach users to have appropriate levels of expectation relative to searching CD-ROM databases.

Librarians have had to be creative in meeting the ever-challenging quandary of funding CD-ROM services. One topic hotly debated these days is whether libraries should charge user fees for accessing CD-ROM databases.

Librarians have also had to spend much time evaluating hardware and software of various CD-ROM products in making collection development decisions.

Librarians have had to handle many side effects of the availability of CD-ROM services in their libraries. CD-ROM use typically leads to an increase in the number of interlibrary loan items requested. One PALINET library reported an increase in the number of requests made by faculty members to start new subscriptions to journals identified in CD-ROM searches. Reference librarians are finding themselves in different roles. Some spend much time simply changing paper in printers, troubleshooting hardware problems, and updating software. Of course, they also have to be available to help users with any searching and retrieval questions.

I think the biggest challenge facing librarians in regard to CD-ROM is simply how to stay on top of this technology. I hope that librarians do not lose that edge of being innovators in this area.

PALINET, along with other networks, also faces many challenges. PALINET staff need to stay on top of current developments to be able to assist libraries in making decisions. Networks can and do play an obvious role in the training arena. Networks need to face the challenge of training the end users. Is this an area into which networks should move? If not, should networks be helping librarians with "train the trainer" workshops?

The vendors and the industry as a whole also have challenges to face. Some of the challenges I perceive actually constitute a wish list. CD-ROM vendors have to continue to adopt standards. The ultimate standard that users and librarians would like to see is the adoption of a standard search interface. Unfortunately, this is not likely to happen, since the search interface is the unique part of each vendor's product. I think that hardware and software prices need to drop. Networking needs to become easier and cheaper. One stumbling block to networking CD-ROM products is the licensing agreement. These hassles need to be examined in an expeditious manner. Remote access into CD-ROM networks needs to be easily accommodated. CD-ROM drives need to become faster and allow faster access time to the discs. Speed would be increased if data were more logically recorded on compact discs.[4] The use of compression technology needs to become more prevalent so that more data can fit on each disc. Believe it or not, some discs are already too small even with over 550 megabytes of storage space available! Tracking software should be developed so that use of CD-ROM products can be easily measured. Menu software would be helpful as well. One PALINET library got tired of waiting for the vendors to develop this software and programmed its own.

Vendors need to overcome fears of losing money through cancellation of print products and decrease in the use of online products. Many libraries report that, if anything, CD-ROM represents an increase in usage of the library. CD-ROM products seem to draw new users into the library. Many of the people who used to request online searches are still doing so. The University of Vermont Medical Library reported a 10 percent drop in the number of online literature searches between 1986 and 1987. However it spent 10 percent more money at the same time.[5] Since most libraries are not cancelling print subscriptions en masse, CD-ROM products do not appear to be having the negative impact so feared by vendors. Obviously more research needs to be done in this area. If my hypothesis could be proven, perhaps vendors might be convinced to lower prices and reduce licensing restrictions.

Let us return to the original question posed by the title of this panel: Has the introduction of CD-ROM technology in libraries represented a revolution or a revolt? There has certainly not been a revolt, but not really a revolution either. Libraries have accepted CD-ROM technology for what it is: simply one more vehicle for information.

NOTES

1. Nancy K. Herther, "How to Evaluate Reference Materials on CD-ROM," *Online* 12 (1988): 106.
2. Paula D. Watson, "Cost to Libraries of the Optical Information Revolution," *Online* 12 (1988): 47.
3. Watson, 46.
4. "Archives in Miniature," *PC Magazine* 8 (1989): 191.
5. Donna Lee, "End User Access to Medline: The Role of CD-ROM," *National Online Meeting: Proceedings of the Ninth National Online Meeting, New York, May 10-12, 1988* (New York: Learned Information, 1988), 202.

Observations on the Use of CD-ROM in Academic Libraries

Joseph A. Michalak

The widespread use of CD-ROM in academic libraries has improved access to information while creating new challenges for users and librarians. To make the best use of these systems, researchers now must intelligently evaluate the wealth of information that they can obtain independently. Accordingly, libraries must deal with the increased demands on collections, services, and staff that are a direct result of making information more accessible to more people.

CD-ROM has significantly changed the way in which library users access information. Patrons have quickly and enthusiastically adopted the technology as an exciting alternative to print and online, appreciating the convenience, ease of use, and greater degree of control over the search process that the medium offers. Undergraduates, in particular, have benefitted from "free" access to CD-ROM. Libraries were quick to adopt CD-ROM as a means of providing computer-based information services to more users than could ever be reached through mediated online searching. At many institutions, the demand for mediated searches—and the demand on librarians' time—has declined after the installation of CD-ROM. As the number of CD-ROM sites grows, libraries increasingly discover that the average cost of a CD-ROM search is less than either mediated searching or end-user services such as DIALOG's Knowledge Index or BRS After Dark.[1,2,3]

For the staff at Hahnemann University, one of the unforeseen benefits of CD-ROM was an improvement in their students' learn-

---

Joseph A. Michalak is Health Sciences Product Manager, SilverPlatter Information, Inc., 303 Potrero Street, Ste. 29-106, Santa Cruz, CA 95060.

© 1990 by The Haworth Press, Inc. All rights reserved.

ing experience: "Since cost is not related to use . . . users can relax and take time to experiment and learn by trial and error, something they do very well. . . . This provides a superior learning environment for students."[4] Unlike online searching, where the continuous "ticking meter" creates a more pressured environment, CD-ROM's fixed cost and unlimited use encourage students to refine search strategies and carefully examine search results. CD-ROM allows institutions to provide the benefits of computer-based search services at a fraction of cost to all users, regardless of status or ability to pay.

IMPACT ON LIBRARY USERS

CD-ROM has made multi-volume indexes such as ERIC and *Psychological Abstracts* more accessible and easier to use. The ability to search many years of data with powerful search techniques at a convenient CD-ROM work station free of charge is an obvious benefit. Now that CD-ROM is a proven technology with work stations commonplace in academic libraries, how has its proliferation affected library users? While it may be too early for definitive answers, some observations can be made based on the comments and concerns of librarians and users.

CD-ROM and computers still have a seductive appeal for students, although student exposure to computers is no longer a novelty, for many come from primary and secondary school environments where computer access is widespread. Within academic libraries, online catalogs with dozens of terminals available for public use have become the rule rather than the exception. Students have few problems adapting to this new technology; in fact, some expect it!

Although CD-ROM is a sophisticated information retrieval tool that can significantly reduce the most laborious and tedious aspects of research, it must be viewed as just one more weapon in the researcher's arsenal. To some extent, however, because of the volume of information that can be retrieved using electronic media, researchers must exercise better judgment and discernment in evaluating the quality of data. Critical evaluation has always been difficult for library users regardless of what means they used to obtain the information. Electronic databases have merely exacerbated this difficulty by making it easier to be overwhelmed by too much data.

Most users would probably be bewildered by a one-minute CD-ROM search that generated 200 references for a five-page term paper. CD-ROM and other electronic media have made the process of gathering data extremely efficient. The user's ability to analyze and evaluate the vast amount of information from these systems, however, has not kept pace. As educators, librarians now must address this imbalance by helping users develop the understanding and discernment needed for more effective exploitation of the data that they find so easily.

IMPACT ON LIBRARY SERVICES AND STAFF

Librarians have always realized that new services create new demands on staff and resources. Bibliographic instruction programs, many of which were introduced in the early 1970s, were designed to enhance academic libraries' usefulness to students. These creative programs were tremendously successful at making libraries a more central part of the educational process on campuses by introducing students to the wealth of available research tools and services. As expected, however, bibliographic instruction had a significant impact on library resources: as students became more sophisticated in the use of information they demanded more services to meet their needs.

CD-ROM has proven to be no exception to that model. Now that CD-ROM has become an indispensable library service, it has created new public service and collection development issues. Libraries have already reported substantial increases in the use of journal collections, inter-library loan services, and microfiche collections, all tied to CD-ROM availability. Increased inter-library loan requests will suggest new collection development directions and more cooperative ventures for shared library resources. As the demand on journal collections increases, the pressure on copyright restrictions will mount until some reasonable way can be found to meet both the legitimate needs of users and the financial demands of publishers.

The introduction of CD-ROM has further challenged staff to become knowledgeable about a variety of operating systems, hardware configurations, software packages, and interface designs. Librarians not only have had to master these complexities well enough to install systems successfully, but also have had to explain them competently to library users. Consider the challenge facing librarians who must explain to a first-time user—someone who may have little subject knowledge—a complex tool like *Psychological Abstracts*. They have to explain both the concept of the resource itself and the technology needed to access the tool. The scope of library practice, once again, has broadened in response to technological advances, leading ultimately to higher standards for entry into the profession.

CD-ROM has also created new opportunities for librarians to interact with faculty and students. The complexity of CD-ROM searching requires librarians to become more involved in user research problems. Librarians are directly challenged to impart their knowledge of information sources and research skills to patrons so that users can cope with the deluge of information and become as self-reliant as possible. Teaching patrons how to use libraries is no longer sufficient. Librarians must refocus the learning process to teach users how to assimilate and evaluate for themselves the information sources for various disciplines.

CONCLUSION

By implementing CD-ROM and other technical innovations designed to improve services, libraries have raised user expectations. Patrons have become more self-sufficient, sophisticated, and demanding. Now libraries are being challenged to find better solutions to the problem of document delivery, solutions that will satisfy patrons and publishers alike. Libraries with large CD-ROM installations are facing heavy demand and are investigating CD-ROM networks. Creative ways must be found to finance CD-ROM databases, computer hardware, and staff to support such operations.

Vendors can help libraries cope with demand. The ability to limit a CD-ROM search to local journal holdings would ensure better use of local resources and less dependence on inter-library loan. Making CD-ROM work stations part of an integrated library system would allow users to query a serial database, generate inter-library loan requests, and generally take fuller advantage of system capabilities. In this age of CD-ROM, academic libraries are moving beyond their traditional functions to play a much larger role in the delivery of information services to the educational system.

NOTES

1. Elena E. Cevallos, Lorraine Palmer, and Charles E. Kratz, "Implementation and Maintenance of End-User CD-ROM Services: An Academic Library's Experience." *Access Faxon* 2 (Summer 1989): 16-22.

2. Vicki Anders and Kathy M. Jackson, "Online vs. CD-ROM—The Impact of CD-ROM Databases Upon a Large Online Searching Program." *Online*, 1988 November, 24-32.

3. Raja Jaytilleke, "CD-ROM: Implications of the Emerging Technology for Academic Information Services," in *Optical Publishing & Storage: Products That Work. Proceedings of Optical Publishing & Storage '87. The Conference on the Application of Optical Information Systems in Publishing* (New York: Learned Information, 1987), 93-101.

4. Carol Hansen Fenichel, "Supporting Users Searching CD-ROM: A Comparison with Online," in *Optical Publishing & Storage: Products That Work. Proceedings of Optical Publishing & Storage '87. The Conference on the Application of Optical Information Systems in Publishing* (New York: Learned Information, 1987), 37-39.

The CD-ROM "Revolution" at Columbia: Year One

Beth Juhl
Anita Lowry

During the 1987/88 academic year, the Columbia University Libraries undertook a study, generously underwritten by the Pew Memorial Trust, of the impact of CD-ROM products and technology on library services and the research process. We evaluated over thirty bibliographic, numeric, and full-text CD-ROMs for content, ease of use, and value to the needs of students and scholars in the Columbia community. In addition, the relative effectiveness of end-user searching in online databases and CD-ROM was compared at three different library sites. We intended these two types of studies to provide basic information about the advantages and disadvantages of the CD-ROM format, their effects on reference services and collection policies, and the implications which new technologies might have for the research process in the humanities, sciences, and social sciences. While the Columbia Libraries have not by any means begun to digest and to address *all* the issues raised by the Pew study, we have been able to use the information gathered during that year in planning for and implementing access to both printed and machine-readable sources in the libraries.

THE COLUMBIA LIBRARIES

Columbia provides an apt environment for a study of a wide range of CD-ROM products. The Columbia library system—to use that hackneyed phrase from travel writing—is "a land of con-

---

Beth Juhl and Anita Lowry are Reference Librarians at Columbia University Libraries, 535 W. 114th Street, Room 316, Butler Library, New York, NY 10027.

© 1990 by The Haworth Press, Inc. All rights reserved.

trasts." More than two dozen libraries are scattered across three campuses. They serve the heterogeneous population typical of most large universities from the freshman composition student to the physician at a metropolitan teaching hospital; however, the proportion of graduate to undergraduate students is unusually high at about three to one. The library system includes separate physics, music, and library science libraries, but no distinct undergraduate library. As part of a decentralized and departmentalized system, each library at Columbia has a "native" population, somewhat skilled if not expert in the reference sources for their own subject area, and a "tourist" class, many of whom may be visiting the library for their first and only time. During the Pew study, we found that many readers were quite willing to travel into unknown territory in search of *PsycLIT* or MEDLINE on compact disc, while they would not have searched out these indexes in their print form.

CD-ROMS STUDIED

Of the thirty-six CD-ROMs which were evaluated, twenty-six were bibliographic databases, most of which correspond in some or all aspects to printed indexes. These included *Art Index, Biography Index, Business Periodicals Index, Cumulative Book Index, General Science Index, Humanities Index, MLA: Modern Language Association International Bibliography, Readers' Guide*, and *Social Sciences Index* from Wilsondisc; CANCER CD, *PsycLIT*, and *Sociofile* from SilverPlatter; *Dissertation Abstracts Ondisc* from University Microfilms; as well as several other indexing and abstracting databases, such as PAIS, *REX: Religious and Theological Abstracts, Books in Print Plus* and *Ulrich's Plus*. Also included were numeric databases such as the Slater Hall *County Statistics* disc; full text databases such as the *Thesaurus Linguae Graecae*; and Datext, which contains statistical, textual, and bibliographic elements. (For a complete list of CD-ROM products studied, see the Appendix.)

EVALUATION METHODS

Each CD-ROM system was evaluated using a combination of questionnaires, observation, and interviews, as well as reports and analysis by librarians and faculty. Though we made an attempt early on to standardize user questionnaires, the number and diversity of products being evaluated, combined with the very different needs and expertise of users of each database, led to some customization for various disciplines. A sample of questions asked includes:

- what sort of information readers were looking for and why it was needed;
- whether or not results were satisfactory;
- what value the CD-ROM had in their research;
- how the CD-ROM compared to the printed index;
- which searching aids were most and least helpful (menus, searching guides, library staff, etc.);
- what were the best and worst features;
- how readers discovered the CD-ROM;
- what they would be willing to pay to search CD-ROMs.

Butler Reference Department, which serves the humanities and history disciplines but also functions as the general reference area for the entire university, received 349 questionnaires from October 1987 to May 1988. Nine CD-ROMs were tested in Butler Reference: eight Wilsonsdisc products including the *MLA*, and *Dissertation Abstracts Ondisc*. We know from our own reference statistics and from sample "head counts" throughout the year that the questionnaires represent less than 10 percent of the total CD-ROM users. The questionnaires were left beside each CD-ROM station, and librarians encouraged readers to fill them out. While recognizing that this was not a controlled, exact method of polling, we wanted to capture quickly a "snapshot" of who was using our CD-ROMs, how the CD-ROMs were being used, and which of the CD-ROMs were getting the most use.

SURVEY RESULTS

It will not come as a surprise that readers *love* CD-ROMs. In Butler Reference, 34 percent of our respondents found that a specific CD-ROM product was *essential* to their research, 75 percent found the CD-ROM version of an index easier to use than its printed counterpart, and 71 percent preferred the CD-ROM format to paper. Our typical survey respondent was a graduate student or upper-division undergraduate looking for books, articles, or dissertations about a specific subject area while working on a research paper, thesis, or term paper. Many of our respondents had never before used a CD-ROM and often were not comfortable with computers. Our promotional efforts (posters, flyers, signs) seemed to have been for naught: most users either stumbled across the machines in the course of their work in the reference room (a good argument for keeping machine-readable and printed formats together) or had CD-ROMs recommended to them by a librarian. Formal training sessions were also disappointing, with less than 15 percent of CD-ROM users taking advantage of short searching classes. Instead, almost all users wanted "on demand" help in beginning their first search, but once they got started, relied on contextual help screens, quick search guides prepared by library staff, or fellow readers.

In short, response to the CD-ROMs in Butler Reference, as elsewhere on campus, was overwhelmingly favorable, even enthusiastic. In written comments and interviews, readers praised the speed, ease of use, convenience, efficiency, and flexibility of CD-ROM searching. The ability to combine terms, to search on keywords or fields not indexed in printed sources, to search cumulations rather than annual volumes, to browse and explore a subject area, and to print citations were all rated as important features. Complaints focused on sometimes difficult or confusing interfaces, on the limited contents of many databases and the lack of retrospective coverage, and on the need for additional CD-ROM stations and discs, especially during peak term paper periods.

While readers *love* CD-ROMs, they do not want to pay for them. Seventy-five percent of the readers in the Butler Reference survey said they would be willing to pay only $5.00 or less, and most readers scoffed at the idea that they should pay anything at all. CD-ROMs were regarded as a service, albeit a wonderful service, that the libraries were obligated to provide free, not billed as another surcharge on top of the already high tuition.

END-USER STUDY

Of course, Boolean operators, keyword and field searching, and even printing, are all features of online searching as well. As a supplement to our general CD-ROM survey, we conducted three studies—one each in the humanities, social sciences, and sciences—in order to compare the mechanics, costs, and comprehensiveness of end-user online searching versus CD-ROM and print sources. In Butler Reference, the *MLA* via Knowledge Index was compared to both the Wilsondisc CD-ROM and printed indexes. In the social sciences, *PsycInfo* via BRS After Dark was compared to SilverPlatter *PsycLit*. In the Math/Science Library, *Science Citation Index* via DIALOG was compared to the Institute for Scientific Information version.

Though it is difficult to weigh these three very dissimilar user populations and indexes against one another, we can make a few general observations about readers' responses to searching in the different formats. Overall, users preferred the CD-ROM or printed index for *browsing* and exploring an index without the pressure of a ticking meter. But, for comprehensive and retrospective searching without confusing menus, disc changes, or limited search options, the online version of a database proved more valuable. Users, once they had been trained in an online system, expressed concerns about the appropriateness of charging for searching, whether on CD-ROM or online. As one student remarked:

> The beauty of this type of resource is that it *allows* more "browsing" in disciplines and databases which WOULD NOT NECESSARILY BE EXPECTED to yield results. This is only true because (a) it is VERY fast, (b) it is relatively easy, and (c) it is FREE. If costs were higher, in time, effort, or money, it would not be as effective in broadening the scope of academic searching.

Cost is indeed an important factor in implementing end-user online searching, as is time. Total online searching costs for the end-user study came to over $2,000 for 83 searches. The same amount would have paid for more than a year of unlimited searching of the

MLA on Wilsondisc. In addition, most end-user database services such as BRS After Dark or Knowledge Index limit searching to evenings and weekends. End-user searching also requires a considerable amount of librarians' time in training users, administering searching schedules, and bookkeeping. Before searching the *MLA* online, users had to attend a two-hour session in order to master system commands on Knowledge Index and the complexities of the *MLA* file itself. Even then, most users needed some online time in order to begin to grasp the *logic* of searching and to formulate effective search strategies. In contrast, readers can walk up to a CD-ROM station in the libraries and, in the words of a colleague, "make the machine move"[1] with a minimum of assistance. It is much easier to plug in a CD-ROM than to train and support hundreds of database searchers.

LIBRARIANS' EVALUATIONS

One of the surveyed users called CD-ROMs "the greatest aid to scholarship since coffee," and librarians were at times only slightly less enthusiastic. Leaving aside for the moment cost and access issues, we found that CD-ROMs brought the power and flexibility of computerized information retrieval to a broad audience in an unintimidating way. Because most of the bibliographic indexes on CD-ROM are cumulative and much less tedious to use than the printed sources, undergraduates—who often do not know any index but the *Readers' Guide*—were particularly attracted to the CD-ROM indexes and used them in more creative and thorough ways. Having the machines visible and clearly labelled on the reference floor attracted readers who may never have encountered the printed sources to which the CD-ROMs corresponded. Once readers got started, usually with a little help from reference staff, they were willing to explore the tools, experiment with search strategies, and thoroughly learn an index—something they would almost never have had the gumption, patience or time to do with a printed tool. The CD-ROMs also turned into public relations machines for the libraries. One or two readers may thank the reference department for acquiring a particularly expensive book set; readers thanked us daily for the "wonderful machines" and perceived the CD-ROMs as something the libraries had done *for* them.

Another advantage of the CD-ROMs was the printouts that readers brought to us with clear, accurate citations to books and journal articles. Those printouts proved to be both a blessing and something of a burden. There was a perceptible jump in interlibrary loan requests for obscure journals not held at Columbia, and some libraries saw increased traffic from new users looking for cited titles. The *General Science Index* in particular produced such a demand for popular science journals that new subscriptions were begun for several of them. The libraries had been receiving the printed *General Science Index* for years, but demand for the journals it indexes escalated dramatically only after we acquired the CD-ROM version. The impact of the CD-ROM version confirmed that more people were discovering and using the *General Science Index* on disc than had ever glanced at the printed tool.

Disadvantages with the CD-ROM format included the expected mechanical problems — paper jams, printer problems, and so forth — of the sort familiar to any librarian who has ever worked in the same building with a photocopy machine. Many of our users were unfamiliar with computers and needed basic help in finding the enter key and getting started, or confused the CD-ROM stations with the online catalog or a word processor. Even those with computer experience had trouble negotiating confusing menu screens and changing discs; the Business Library lost two discs when readers put them into the floppy drive.

The "magic" aura of the computer resulted in an undiscriminating attitude toward search results in some instances. Students were unwilling to switch to an old-fashioned paper source even when the CD-ROM tool was inappropriate for their topic, or to supplement their printouts with printed sources. As Christine Borgmann has written, "We need to be careful to distinguish between approval of these systems by library patrons and the actual effectiveness of their use."[2] This, however, is a problem that reference librarians have encountered all along with traditional tools: we cannot guarantee that every bibliography or index will be used effectively or appropriately by every reader. Some readers will use CD-ROMs intelligently and creatively and some will not, but most *think* their use of the CD-ROM a success and want to use it over and over again.

IMPLICATIONS FOR SERVICES, RESOURCES, AND ACCESS

From October 1987 to May 1988, the Butler Reference Desk alone received more than 2300 CD-ROM related questions. Student assistants and interns can handle much of the day-to-day mechanical care and feeding of CD-ROM workstations, and system improvements and the learning curve of repeat users may eventually decrease the sheer volume of questions we receive. But CD-ROMs will never be labor-saving devices. CD-ROM users want "on demand" assistance from reference staff, from handouts and user guides, or from the system itself; most will not avail themselves of any training classes. At the same time, advanced bibliographic instruction is needed for upper-level undergraduate and graduate students, as well as faculty, to provide them with a conceptual framework for making intelligent use of all reference sources, and for integrating CD-ROMs into their own research routines. As always, librarians are called upon by students and scholars for help in negotiating this plethora of information sources, and CD-ROMs require a renewed commitment on the part of reference librarians to their role as instructor and consultant.

Perhaps the greatest impediment to the use of CD-ROMs is their cost. Trying to make broad generalizations about the price of CD-ROMs compared to the price of their printed counterparts is like trying to compare apples and oranges — or perhaps a better analogy is raspberries and oranges — since CD-ROM is undeniably more expensive than print (with a few exceptions). While they may be more expensive than traditional reference tools, CD-ROMs are completely different resources that mark a major advance in reference service by providing ready access to computerized information retrieval, without many of the disadvantages of online systems.

The preliminary figure for renewing all the CD-ROMs chosen for a second year of evaluation at Columbia was over $35,000. Costs of equipment, furniture, security devices, maintenance, and staffing must be figured in as well. Though industry pricing is not yet stable, and competition may cause some prices to fall, cancellation of printed sources alone will not pay for the CD-ROM "revolution." In truth, the libraries have too many unanswered questions about multi-user access and the long-term prognosis for CD-ROMs as an archival medium to begin throwing out other formats. Nor would raiding our database searching budget or charging the users be viable alternatives. While we like to claim that CD-ROMs are just like any other reference tool, and that users should have free and easy access to all the sources necessary to their research, we do not want CDs to come out of our already tight book and serial budgets. The budgeting debate is ongoing across the country, and at Columbia we are already beginning what will probably be many years of trade-offs and compromises.[3]

By far the biggest drawback to CD-ROMs apart from cost is the problem of only one user per disc. Though Local Area Network (LAN) technology holds great promise, it is a day-to-day fact that more readers can simultaneously make use of a printed source. We have tried not to limit searching time or implement sign-up schedules for our CD-ROMs. Readers are for the most part gracious and self-policing, but they do become testy around term paper time.

Because of the already high demand, it may be just as well that CD-ROMs are not listed in the online catalog, but the growth of materials in machine-readable format will at some point necessitate the addition of data files to the catalog. Anna Wang[4] has discussed some of the difficulties of cataloging CD-ROM products: lack of standards in bibliographic information, updates and revisions of software, and linking print and disc titles. With a library system as complex as Columbia's, however, we cannot expect users to stumble across the CD-ROM sources that suit their needs.

A YEAR LATER

Columbia has chosen to renew the majority of our original thirty-six CD-ROMs for a second year, and we have added several newly released or test systems as well. While bibliographic databases seem to have found a home in many of the reference departments across campus, full-text and numeric CD-ROMs have presented more problems in terms of access and training. To cope with the increased instructional and outreach services required to keep our readers abreast of technological advances, the libraries have recently opened an Electronic Reference Center, which will present courses, demonstrations, and workshops on CD-ROM and other machine-readable sources. Several libraries continue to offer end-user online searching in addition to their CD-ROM systems. The title of our panel this morning is "Revolution or Revolt." I am afraid that, while CD-ROMs have caused some sweeping changes in services and resources at Columbia, we are in the middle of an ongoing evolution, not a revolution. And the only revolt I foresee is that of the readers if we should try to take the CD-ROMs away.

NOTES

1. Deborah Bezanson, "Integrating CD-ROM with Printed and Online Services: A SilverPlatter End-User Perspective," *Optical Information Systems* 7 (November/December 1987): 389.

2. Christine L. Borgmann, "Information Retrieval from CD-ROM: Status Quo or a Revolution in End-User Access?" The *Canadian Journal of Information Science* 12 no. 3/4 (1987): 51.

3. See Kathleen Coleman and Linda Muroi, "The Reference Department Budget in the High Tech Era: An Endangered Species?" *Reference Librarian* 19 (1987): 137-157.

4. Anna Wang, "Cataloging CD-ROMS at the Ohio State University," *Serials Review* 14 no. 3 (1988): 11-21.

Appendix: List of CD-ROMs Studied at Columbia

Database	Type
Art Index (Wilson)	Bibliographic
Biography Index (Wilson)	Bibliographic
Books in Print Plus & Ulrich's Plus (Bowker)	Bibliographic
Business Indicators Disk (Slater Hall)	Numeric
Business Periodicals Index (Wilson)	Bibliographic
Cancer-CD (SilverPlatter)	Bibliographic
Compact Cambridge MEDLINE (Cambridge Scientific Abstracts)	Bibliographic
Compustat PC Plus (Standard & Poor's)	Numeric, Textual
County Statistics Disk (Slater Hall)	Numeric
Cumulative Book Index (Wilson)	Bibliographic
DATEXT (Lotus Development Corp.)	Bibliographic, Textual, Numeric
Dissertation Abstracts Ondisc (University Microfilms Int'l.)	Bibliographic
Earthquake Digital Data (US Geological Survey)	Numeric
General Science Index (Wilson)	Bibliographic
Geobase WORM (Lamont Doherty Geological Observatory)	Numeric, Graphic
Humanities Index (Wilson)	Bibliographic
"LE PAC" Government Document Option (Brodart)	Bibliographic
MLA International Bibliography (Wilson)	Bibliographic

McGraw-Hill CD-ROM Science and Technical Reference Set (McGraw-Hill)	Full-text
PAIS on CD-ROM (PAIS, Inc)	Bibliographic
PC-SIG Library on CD-ROM (PC-SIG)	Public domain software
PsycLIT (SilverPlatter)	Bibliographic
Readers' Guide to Periodical Literature (Wilson)	Bibliographic
REX: Religious and Theological Abstracts (FABS Int'l, Inc.)	Bibliographic
Science Citation Index (Institute for Scientific Information)	Bibliographic
Search CD450 Database: NTIS (OCLC)	Bibliographic
Sociofile (SilverPlatter)	Bibliographic
Thesaurus Linguae Graecae (TLG, University of California, Irvine)	Full-text
PHI Demonstration Disk (Packard Humanities Index)	Full-text
U. S. National Atlas (Geovision)	Graphic

DEPARTMENT STORES TO BOUTIQUES: HOW MANY SERIALS VENDORS AND WHAT KIND OF SERVICES DOES YOUR LIBRARY NEED?

Determining Which Subscription Agency Services Best Meet Your Needs

N. Bernard "Buzzy" Basch

My experience is in large U.S. subscription agencies offering comprehensive "department store" services—agencies such as EBSCO, Faxon, Readmore, McGregor, and Majors—rather than the "boutique" agencies such as Harrassowitz which provide specialized services or services tailored to the needs of a specialized customer base. In contrast with the individualized approaches of the "boutiques," the "department store" agencies have large regional or centralized offices, offer a common set of services, and compete on pricing, perceptions of service quality, and the promotion of a corporate image designed to appeal to libraries of all types and sizes.

Although department store agencies stress the unique characteris-

---

N. Bernard "Buzzy" Basch was formerly Vice President of EBSCO Subscription Services. He currently resides at 860 N. Lake Shore Drive, Chicago, IL 60611.

© 1990 by The Haworth Press, Inc. All rights reserved.

tics of their individual services, there is little difference among the range of services that they support. All offer order placement; internal automation; consolidated payment, administration, and claiming; online access to files of bibliographic and publisher information; reports and invoices customized to client needs; access to historic pricing data; machine-readable data for local system input; generation of kardex labels; and the use of toll-free telephone lines. Some companies have developed distinctive auxiliary services such as serials updating bulletins, missing copy banks, proprietary serials check-in software, union listing systems, and access to files of MARC cataloging records. Nonetheless, the common core of services is available through all large vendors, although the vendors may package the services in different ways.

A library can readily determine whether all or part of its subscription needs can best be fulfilled by a boutique agency. The more significant decision comes in choosing which of multiple department store agencies will provide the best non-boutique service.

If the department stores offer essentially the same services, what is the determining factor in the selection of an agent? Price, the image that the agency chooses to promote, or the personality of the local sales representative? Conventional wisdom argues for a focus on price, a focus that I would be the last person to dispute. Price is, however, relative. The lowest cost service is not necessarily what best meets the needs of a particular library, and price is negotiable, often depending on the services used by a library. Agency services are not always as identical or significant as we assume. A responsible selection decision requires close examination of a library's specific needs and the services that each candidate agency offers to meet these needs.

To illustrate the evaluation and assessment of library needs and the services that vendors provide to fulfill these needs, consider the claiming of missing issues. We all assume that subscription agency support for claiming is a valuable service, but this assumption is not valid in some circumstances. An agent's support for claiming is of no benefit to a library that has neither the staff nor the system resources to recognize the non-receipt of journal issues. Nor may agency claiming be of value to a library for which *immediate* follow-up is critical. The fastest way to replace missing issues is to claim directly from the publisher. This entails direct costs for a library—labor, research to verify the publisher's address, postage, and phone tolls—but offers the most rapid resolution of the missing issue problem.

Agency versus direct claiming are the two extremes of the claiming spectrum. The needs of most libraries fall somewhere in the middle, a ground in which agency claiming support services have some attraction by reducing direct costs to the library and by achieving a relatively satisfactory and speedy response. Most of the large agencies offer some degree of electronic support for claiming but, again, it is necessary to examine and assess common assumptions about the extent, effectiveness, and cost of such services. In some cases, electronic support for claiming achieves little other than affording library staff a rosy glow of satisfaction at being in the mainstream of technological development; but the tangible benefits may be no greater than those provided by an agent's multi-part forms for manual reporting of claims.

Electronic claims must be keyed by library staff (unless the library uses an automated serials control system that automatically identifies claim situations, generates claim reports, *and* provides an electronic interface to transfer the claims to the agent's claiming system). Once entered, claim data are transmitted to the agency, one hopes over toll-free telephone lines. The electronic claims reach the agency more quickly than would hardcopy reports sent through the mail.

We assume that electronic claims are processed more quickly, but this is not a valid assumption. Some electronic claim systems are nothing more than electronic mail. The claims transmitted from libraries are either processed manually or re-keyed into the agency's automated system by vendor staff. And agencies' automated systems vary in their claim generation and tracking capabilities: some produce only printed claims whereas others support the generation of electronic claims to publishers. If speed of claiming is significant in a specific library situation, the actual operation of the electronic claim systems of the contending vendors should be explored in some detail. If vendor staff re-key the claims into an internal system, what is the agent's target for re-keying turnaround? How is performance against this objective monitored? How frequently are claims processed by the vendor's system: daily, weekly, or every other week? And once processed, how often are claims dispatched? How many claims are bundled to a publisher at one time? (Similar questions are relevant for electronic ordering capabilities if these are judged to be of significance in a particular library's operations.)

As in all aspects of serials management, there is a third party to be considered: the publisher. Only a few publishers have the ability to accept electronic orders, let alone claims. The publishers of high circulation magazines or very expensive titles generally have sophisticated in-house circulation systems, or use fulfillment agencies with such systems. These systems do not necessarily accept orders or claims in electronic format. In practice, the level of publisher support for electronic claiming is so low as to defuse the significance of an agency's ability to generate electronic claims. However, this reality is not necessarily clear when a library is compiling its short list of essential agency support services or comparing the claim support of competing vendors.

These are just some of the issues involved in subscription agency support for claiming. If claiming is critical to the mission of a specific library, it is important to delve through assumptions, examine what each agency offers, and consider the effectiveness of the service in terms of the library's specific needs. If one agency offers services or execution significantly better suited to the needs of the library, the library should determine whether there is a price differential for this superior performance. Is the service worth this price? (Pricing differentials are unlikely to be expressed in terms of specific charges for specific services, but rather bundled in the overall service charge for the account.) Conversely, if a library situation is such that its claiming needs are best met by direct claims to publishers, can non-use of the agency's claiming support be a negotiating point to reduce the service charge?

The service and handling charges levied by department store agencies depend upon a number of factors, the most significant being the mix of titles ordered by a library, the dollar volume of the account, and the margin of discount that the agent receives from the publisher. Some agents also have specific charges for certain services such as transaction charges for additional orders or the mailing and billing of continuations. An agency's perception of the marketplace can also be significant. Marketing to a library in Springfield is very different from marketing to a library in midtown Manhattan, and marketing to a small public library is different from marketing to an ARL library. An agency will determine charges within a continuum established by its perception of what the market will bear.

In addition to direct service charges—the difference between the total cost of a library's subscriptions and the total of the agent's invoice—a library should also be aware of hidden service costs that relate to the cost of money. If a library pays its invoice in June and the agency does not remit payments to publishers until the end of October, the agency receives free use of the money for four months. At a prime rate of eleven and a half percent, this is approximately one percent per month, for a total of four percent for four months. On an invoice of $100,000 this represents a "cost" to the library of $4,000. Once recognized, this aspect of the service charge can be reduced by negotiating for an appropriate pre-payment discount.

Whether a library chooses to avail itself of all of the services offered by a vendor, it is important to determine which services are critical to the operations of the library, which vendor offers the best support for such essential functions, and to negotiate for the required services at an acceptable price.

The Serials Acquisition Partnership

Jane Maddox

As I started preparing for this conference, I was reminded of a quotation I have noticed hanging on the office walls of several of the serials departments I have visited over the years: "When you are up to your (you-know-what) in alligators, it is hard to remember that the original purpose was to drain the swamp."

And, as I thought about traversing the swampland of Serialdom, this brought to mind a political joke I heard recently: Have you heard about the latest gaffe of one of our infamous politicians? He thought Roe vs. Wade was a reference to the crossing of the Delaware!

While we certainly will not find any alligators in the Delaware, if you are in a swamp, there are definite advantages to rowing versus wading.

If you will bear with me, I would like to take this metaphor one step further as I address the topic for this panel discussion, "department store" versus "boutique" serials vendors. My basic premise is that the library and the serials vendor are partners in one small function of the process of providing access to information, namely, serials acquisitions, and that professional conduct on the part of both partners is necessary in order to maintain the high standards that move a profession forward.

Or, to put it another way, depending upon what each of the partners brings to the process of serials acquisitions, we can all be in the boat rowing through the higher levels of the swamp; we can be "taken for a ride" if we are not doing our share of rowing; or,

Jane Maddox has been a North American Representative for Otto Harrassowitz since 1978. Her current mailing address is P.O. Box 10, Columbia, MD 21045-0010.

© 1990 by The Haworth Press, Inc. All rights reserved.

indeed, we may be wading through the lower levels of the swamp, up to our (you-know-what) in alligators.

Now many of the same *kinds* of services are offered by both department store-type and boutique-type serial vendors. The obvious differences are a broader range of products from the department store-type and a smaller, more specialized range of products from the boutique-type. I will not elaborate further about specific services because I know that my colleagues on the panel will be going into greater detail on that topic.

Since the serials acquisition process engages the library in a trade relationship with a partner, *how* the business is conducted is at least equally important as what services are required. How a company does business is reflected in their marketing and sales policies and practices. It is this area that I will want to discuss in more detail.

There has always been a great deal of discussion as to why it is so important for serials vendor professionals to have an in-depth knowledge of library serials acquisition policies and procedures. However, it is just as incumbent on library professionals to have in-depth knowledge of how serials vendors conduct their business. It is only with this knowledge and understanding that we can ensure that high standards, worthy of our profession, are employed as we conduct the business of serials acquisitions.

Before I begin to examine some of the differences in marketing and sales policies for department store and boutique serials vendors, some further clarification and disclaimers are in order. October Ivins introduced me as having worked primarily for the boutique-type vendor. However, to put this in perspective, you should be aware that even the smallest vendor with which I have been associated employed about 100 people; and in my present situation, there are over 250 employees. So when I refer to a "boutique," I am not talking about a "mom and pop" operation. I am going to use the extremes to contrast the large business versus the small, but I fully recognize that most companies are somewhere in between. Also, I will be making generalizations, and yet I am fully aware that there are exceptions to any generalization. All I can say is, "If the shoe fits, wear it!"

A big first concern in marketing for any company is market definition: the customers to be served and the services to be provided.

The boutique approach acknowledges that there is room for competitors, since the market is a well-defined, moderately small area, usually with a high degree of specialization.

The large business has a more far-reaching definition of its market, often global. Comprehensiveness and specialization of services are more difficult to achieve within this larger area. Rather than acknowledging competitors, it is not uncommon for large businesses to develop marketing strategies for the elimination of competitors. They achieve this by buying out the competition. We certainly have seen a lot of this happening in recent years. But it is probably more often achieved in a way that I saw described in an article recently about the real-estate tycoon Trammell Crow, from Texas. In its quest for market share, his company drives prices down to the point that no one, not even the company itself, can make money in that particular market sector. The assumption here is that the company can temporarily use profits from other markets to offset losses in this market, whereas, they hope, other smaller firms with less diversification cannot, would ultimately suffer from the loss, and eventually be eliminated.

While the lowering of prices in this approach to market share definition may appear to the consumer to be a positive event, in the long run it could ultimately result in higher prices because of a lack of competition. In this same article about Crow and his company, the writers point out that the bid process can be a perfect vehicle for eliminating competition.

Once the market is defined, companies usually try to reach that market through advertising. Much advertising by large businesses can be grouped under one heading: manipulation. This type of advertising as defined by the Madison Avenue approach usually tries to take advantage of some basic human insecurities or to introduce some gimmick that will entice you to do something you would not have done otherwise. As a general consumer, I am insulted by this type of advertising in the general trade. As a professional participant in the information industry, I am appalled by some of the advertising and marketing gimmicks I see being used today. So far, we have stopped short of the "free toaster if you will open an account" approach, but we are not far from it. Gimmicks or incentives only designed to bring in new business are suspect at best. Did you ever ask yourself, "Why are they wanting to compensate me for doing business with them?" How equitable is it for only new customers to get some special compensation? What about those loyal customers who have been doing business with them for years? If a company can afford to give back money, why take it in the first place? Why not just lower prices to all customers?

One of the more recent large business advertising schemes actually gets you to do the marketing research for the firm and at the same times keeps you away from the competitors. I am sure you have all seen the Sears, Montgomery Wards, or Walmart ads pledging to match any advertised sale price. Great! There was a time when the companies did their own marketing research to find out what their competitors were doing. Now the consumer is providing them with that information. But what price is paid by the general consumer who did not happen to see an advertised sale price? Once again, if the company can afford to sell at the lower price, they should do just that and then offer an equitable price for all customers.

Surely this sort of thing would never happen in this profession! I am afraid it does. Libraries have received refunds from vendors when the vendor was presented with information on lower prices from another vendor, and vendors have promised to match the prices of a vendor providing lower prices. If the vendor could afford to refund money, why collect it in the first place? If the vendor is going to match the other vendor's lower prices for this particular library, what about the prices charged to other libraries? How is the library going to be sure that the vendor is keeping its promise by matching the prices offered by the other vendors?

Are these the high standards for conducting business that we want for our profession?

In discussions with various librarians, I have asked how they feel about the advertising and marketing schemes that are being used by various serials vendors. The responses I have received can be summed up in the following statement.

Ever mindful of the professionals they serve, serials vendors, regardless of size, should refrain from using the slick, Madison Avenue manipulative advertising and, instead, strive to provide information aimed at increasing levels of awareness and understanding of professional concerns.

Some libraries have gone so far as to develop rules governing business transactions, in order to avoid becoming a partner in marketing schemes designed specifically to bring in immediate sales for the serials vendor and only short-term benefits for the library. Basically, the rules state that if something is offered by a vendor that is not printed in widely distributed brochures, and if it is not an incentive available to all customers, the library cannot enter into the agreement.

Moving from marketing now to examine differences in sales policies and procedures, we will look at the point of contact for the sales transaction within the company, which usually is a sales representative.

In the area of sales, the boutique approach is usually very personalized. Often the owner is involved directly in the sales procedures, or if not, has immediate management control over the sales personnel who represent the firm. With the direct involvement of the owner, there is a great deal of emphasis on the quality of representation. The close working relationship emphasizes continuous training to increase the representative's knowledge and understanding of exactly what the company is doing and how it relates to the industry as a whole.

When I shop at a boutique-type store I usually come away not only with my purchase, but also with some new knowledge as well. For example: the owner of the small stereo shop where we bought our amplifier and tuner not only told us all about what we bought but also described the pros and cons of other brands as well, even some he did not sell. In addition, he diagnosed what was wrong with our car speakers just by hearing us describe the problem. When we looked for stereo equipment at the department store, it was difficult to get any information other than a standard sales pitch.

When I first started out in the library industry over fifteen years ago, I had my library degree, but no experience. I went through the basic training course for the vendor I was to represent and set out to bring in sales. While I did know some things, my basic problem was that I was not aware that I did not know everything.

Since the vendor I was representing had recently defined its market as "supplying everything the academic library needed," how could I go wrong? When one of the first libraries I visited inquired about our ability to supply children's books, I confidently asserted that we could. What I did not know and did not state was that we did not supply these from stock and that, therefore, the delivery time would be slower than from a company that did supply from stock. Also, if I had known more about particular publishers' idiosyncrasies, I could have clarified the situation even further, so that the library would have had realistic expectations of our services, or might even have decided not to use our services at all.

Now clearly, I was not bringing professional expertise to this relationship (although I did have a professional library degree). But the library should have called my bluff! Had they asked probing questions, we both would have quickly become aware that I did not know what I was talking about. I could have gotten answers and reported back to the library, and we all would have learned something in the process. Or, if the company which I was representing had recognized that I would meet with probing questions, perhaps it would have invested in more training or have tailored its services to provide what it could do best. Unfortunately, some organizations tend to emphasize quantity of sales, sometimes at the expense of quality of sales.

If both partners in this trade relationship are conducting themselves in a professional manner, providing as well as seeking accurate information to enhance our knowledge, we will both continue to grow and move the profession forward. This is what we should strive for regardless of the size of the serials vendor, and in this process we will all be doing a lot more rowing and less wading. We might even be able to drain the swamp!

Order Consolidation: A Shift to Single Vendor Service

Jan Anderson

Utah State University's Merrill Library houses a serials collection of approximately 6,000 current titles concentrated largely in science and technology. About 4,600 of these titles are paid subscriptions, with a value of approximately $850,000. For many years U.S.U. acquired these serials primarily from two domestic vendors; several years ago we added one European vendor.

U.S.U.'s serials budget has been strained in recent years by inflation. In the summer of 1986, the library's Executive Director instructed the Serials Department to investigate the possibility of savings through consolidation of serial orders with a single vendor. Following the investigation, U.S.U. did consolidate orders, and we have been pleased with the outcome. I would like briefly to discuss this change and its benefits.

The Serials Department initially resisted the suggestion of vendor consolidation. Staff had recently completed a conversion from visible file check-in to automated serials records using the GEAC Integrated Library System and was reluctant to re-process thousands of records for a vendor change. In addition, we believed that ongoing competition between our two domestic vendors was beneficial to the library. Our policy was to place new orders with the company that was presently giving us better service. Since, however, library administrators were firmly committed to dollar savings, serials staff agreed to investigate the possibilities.

The first step was an informal telephone survey of six college and university libraries, each of which had consolidated orders with one

---

Jan Anderson is Head of Serials and Current Periodicals, Merrill Library, UMC 3000, Utah State University, Logan, UT 84322-3000.

© 1990 by The Haworth Press, Inc. All rights reserved.

or the other of our domestic vendors. The names of these libraries were supplied by the vendors and presumably represented some of their most satisfied customers. Two striking facts emerged from the survey: (1) five of the six libraries had changed vendors because of service problems with another company; and (2) five of the six indicated that their libraries had realized no significant savings from the consolidation. They suggested that changing was not worth the effort unless we were experiencing service problems.

In spite of this information, we decided to proceed with a detailed Request for Proposal (or RFP) to discover exactly what services might be gained and how much money might be saved through consolidation.

As Head of Serials, it was my job to prepare, with committee input, an RFP which would give us enough information to decide whether order consolidation would be beneficial, and if so, which vendor should receive our combined business. The final RFP included eighty items and asked questions ranging from how many of U.S.U.'s titles the vendors could supply, to what support the vendors would give us for the record conversion process. Every query and request we had was included. We even asked whether the vendors would guarantee delivery of claimed issues within a specified number of days.

Next came the problem of deciding to whom we should send the Request for Proposal. We assumed that our present two domestic vendors would be the primary competitors for our orders, but we did not want to overlook any company which might be interested in making an offer. We finally sent our RFP to the six vendors which the 1986 edition of Bowker's *Magazine Industry Market Place* listed as capable of supplying over 100,000 serial titles. Three of these six companies responded with detailed answers to our RFP and packets of supporting information. Two of the three were our own domestic vendors.

Our final information-gathering step was a formal telephone survey of ten libraries, also satisfied customers of the various vendors. We asked questions about collection size, service charge rate, and service satisfaction. We added the librarians' answers to the vendors' RFP responses and forwarded all documentation to a committee.

Committee members used a score sheet to quantify their evaluations. After deliberation and consultation, the committee decided that order consolidation would in fact benefit the library and indicated their choice of vendor. Beginning January 1, 1988, the chosen vendor took over all of the U.S.U. serial orders that they could supply.

For U.S.U., the results of this order consolidation have been overwhelmingly positive. But first let me cover the less desirable results. One real regret was the loss of an amazing account executive who had provided us with outstanding service for a number of years. Another concern is that a year and a half after consolidation our account with the domestic vendor we left is still not completely closed, primarily because of delayed 1987 publications.

The most troublesome aspect of the project was the conversion process itself. The GEAC printout which we provided to the chosen vendor was not sufficiently clear for their purposes. Because the printout was generated from acquisitions records rather than from catalog records, the truncated title lines sometimes contained former titles or routing notes instead of verified titles. If our serials catalog had been online at the time, we could have produced a printout which would have saved ourselves and the vendor a great deal of agony.

We are still receiving duplicate issues of some titles. Since the vendor agreed in the RFP to bear the cost of any duplicates (and a few have been expensive), the dollar loss is theirs, but the effort is still costing us staff time and frustration.

Another problem resulted from my personal lack of serials experience. After we had made the consolidation decision, the chosen vendor contacted publishers while we awaited the arrival of the many renewal invoices. Unbeknownst to me, our former European vendor does not send renewal invoices but requires the customer to notify them, unprompted, of any changes. Our resulting late notification of this vendor cost both the vendor and ourselves money and aggravation. Were it not for our substantial monographic trade with that company, I suspect the error would have cost us a great deal more.

Like myself, our bookkeeper was new at her job. In her enthusiasm to learn her new assignment she paid the renewal invoice which we received from one of our domestic vendors before the vendor selection process was complete. Luckily for us, the company caught our mistake and telephoned to ask whether we really wanted them to cash our check; we did not. We are grateful to both of the vendors we abandoned for their assistance.

Then there was the little matter of the oh's and the zeroes. Our in-house serials order numbers all begin with zero-A, for a reason now lost in the mists of time. A data entry clerk for our chosen vendor mis-keyed a thousand of these as oh-A rather than zero-A, and our GEAC system, not recognizing the numbers, refused to allow us to pay for any of these titles.

Perhaps the only comfort we can draw from these and other glitches, large and small, is that most are behind us. We now have almost all the titles entered correctly. If service from our chosen vendor deteriorates, or if the service charge climbs, future vendor switches should be much easier. Our initial concern about eliminating the competition provided by our split order arrangement is more than balanced by the realization that, while any problems we have with the vendor may now affect all our orders, the same vendor is now in a position to *lose* all our orders.

Now for the positive results. The original goal of consolidation was savings in service charges. Our new service charge rate is less than half the composite amount we were previously paying to the three separate vendors. Accordingly, in the first year of the change, U.S.U. saved approximately $17,500 in service charges alone. In years when the university budget office allows us to prepay, the interest earned through the vendor's prepayment plan could cover our service charge fees at the new rate. As agreed in the RFP response, we are guaranteed this lower service charge for three years and the same rate or lower for the following three years.

The second area of anticipated savings was staff time. Before the consolidation, we split our paid orders among three vendors (who respectively handled 40 percent, 24 percent, and 4 percent of our business) and ordered the remaining 32 percent direct. After the consolidation, our chosen vendor supplies 80 percent of our titles, and we order 20 percent direct. The resulting conveniences are significant: 80 percent of our titles are now covered in every vendor-supplied management report. We now deal with a single sales representative and a single account executive. In addition, the vendor picked up more than 500 of our previously direct orders. The resulting time savings in correspondence, claiming, and invoice-processing easily pays for the service charge we incurred when the vendor took over these titles.

The vendor supplies us with GEAC-loadable invoice tapes which, although they still must be checked against paper copies, save us hours of keying. In addition, the consolidation of orders reduces by at least half the number of these invoice tapes. Testing of online claims transmittal from our GEAC system to the vendor has also begun. The vendor's commitment to developing GEAC interfaces is clearly demonstrated by these innovations and was one factor in the consolidation deliberations.

A further benefit of our new library-vendor relationship is that we are now a large account. Whatever the more subtle attentions this fact no doubt brings to us, it should also carry some weight when we renegotiate our service charge.

Would Utah State University recommend that other libraries consolidate their serials orders with a single vendor? Maybe. Would we recommend investigating the possibilities? Definitely. Whether because of the length of our title list or the size of our budget, three vendors found the prospect of winning our whole account attractive enough to make appealing offers. We believe that using a detailed Request for Proposal and quantifying our evaluations of RFP responses resulted in significant dollar savings and valuable improvements in services.

We Need Department Store *and* Boutique Serials Vendors

October Ivins

My experience in two large research libraries has been that multiple serials vendors—both department stores and boutiques—are needed. I will be addressing my remarks to fellow serials managers, but I hope that others in the audience will find them of interest as well. I will first outline the philosophy or reasons for using multiple vendors. Next, I will discuss the circumstances under which existing vendor assignment would be questioned, and some situations when a vendor cannot or should not be used. Following these introductory comments, I will describe ideas for evaluating factual and subjective information about present vendor use. Next, the decision process for determining how many and which vendors to employ will be considered. In conclusion, I will discuss planning and implementing a project of vendor reassignment.

PHILOSOPHY/REASONS

In considering this subject, I came up with six reasons to use multiple vendors.

1. The variety of materials and publishers makes it unlikely than any one vendor can handle all titles equally well.
2. Using multiple vendors avoids the financial risk of "putting all of one's eggs in one basket."
3. I feel a personal responsibility to foster competition. This is

October Ivins is Head of Serials Services, Louisiana State University, Troy H. Middleton Library, Baton Rouge, LA 70803.

perhaps selfish, but I want to continue to have a choice of vendors in the future.
4. Vendors have differing strengths and weaknesses, and it is possible to identify these.
5. One's ability to compare performance and services offered is enhanced.
6. As long as the potential for increased business exists, one's library will receive better service.

TIMES TO QUESTION VENDOR ASSIGNMENT

There are many occasions or opportunities to question or evaluate vendor assignment. I think such evaluation should be ongoing, but four occasions seem to be the most common in provoking evaluation.

1. New job: when one moves to another library, or has serials vendor assignment added to existing responsibilities in the same library.
2. Dissatisfaction: when one is dissatisfied with the present vendor assignment and/or performance. (It is assumed that the present vendor has been informed and that attempts to resolve problems have been unsatisfactory.)
3. Library changes: internal changes in the library may alter what is desired from a vendor. For example, if the library installs a new automated system, vendor-produced management reports may not be needed.
4. Vendor viability: when vendor viability is lessened as evidenced by financial, management or performance difficulties, use of the vendor should be reevaluated.

RESTRICTIONS

There may be institutional or administrative restrictions on the amount of independence the serials manager exercises in vendor selection. For example,

1. The library may be required to bid for services.
2. There may be a formal or informal mandate, from the funding source or library administration, to consider a single factor (such as price, or service charge) as the sole factor in vendor selection.
3. Prior contracts or agreements may limit flexibility.
4. Preferences at higher administrative levels may restrict choices.

If factors such as these produce a situation in which vendor selection is not optimum, it is the serials manager's responsibility to challenge the factors restricting selection.

EXCEPTIONS

One should keep in mind that not every title should or can be ordered through a vendor. For example, titles that may receive better service or a lower price without a vendor are fulfillment center titles; memberships and other package subscriptions which are not available through vendors; consistently delayed publications, when direct monitoring avoids payment years in advance of supply; and any other "problem" situation in which the library must consistently deal directly with the publisher. Some types of titles cannot be ordered through vendors, such as leased services or titles issued under exclusive distribution arrangements.

LIBRARY ASSESSMENT/FACTUAL

The first stage in evaluating vendor assignment is to determine in as much detail as possible the current vendor profiles. How many vendors are in use? For each vendor, how many titles are on order? What is the dollar value of the annual account? What service charge is assessed?

Information that is more difficult to compile but equally useful is the type and volume of material ordered from each vendor. What types of serials are ordered: periodicals, irregular titles, monographic series? What types of publishers are handled: commercial, small press, amateur, academic department, governmental, societies (where the address may change annually)? In which countries are the publishers located: United States, Europe, Third World? (If this information is not readily available from library sources, some vendors can provide "country of origin" breakdowns for the titles on order with them.)

Another aspect of this evaluation is to identify any particular collection strengths of the library. It may be that a boutique vendor is available but not being used for materials in special subject or geographical areas.

LIBRARY ASSESSMENT/SUBJECTIVE

This category has a direct tie-in with vendor performance evaluation, but addressing that topic would require another talk or another fifteen minutes![1] Briefly, serials vendor performance evaluation is not yet well developed. Some of these categories include objective or quantifiable information, but since the ability to quantify such information is not widely available, I include them in subjective information. For now, trying to determine vendor performance in broad categories by subjective means (if that is all that is available) is still better than not evaluating performance at all. Subjective means can include informal sampling, talking to staff who observe vendor performance, and other informal methods.

A 1985 survey by Derthick and Moran of vendor selection in Association of Research Libraries members found four key factors: prompt renewals, accurate invoices, speedy claims, and rapid placement of orders. Also significant were serials' country of origin and agent experience.[2] The top four show that the old standbys have retained their importance. I group the items I examine in vendor performance into four categories.

1. Fulfillment, which includes order entry, claiming and renewal.
2. Price, including base price and service charges. This category acknowledges that vendors do not simply charge a base price set by publishers, and that paying a reasonable service charge on moderate base prices can be more cost-effective than paying a smaller service charge on inflated prices.

3. Communication, which considers the ease and effectiveness of communicating with the vendor. Are responses forthcoming without follow-up by the library? Does the vendor supply advance notification of changes of titles, publishers, addresses and so forth?
4. Intelligence/ability, which is a "grab bag" including other areas of service. Can the vendor accommodate local requirements, such as printing a correctly formatted order number for each title? Can fund codes be listed on invoices and summarized to speed payment authorization? Are the vendor supplied management reports accurate and useful? Does the vendor screen claims for accuracy or simply forward them to the publisher? Do you have to suggest solutions or actions, or can the customer service staff make such determinations (i.e., "This is a third claim for a lapsed title. Please supply proof of payment.")? Are orders screened or just entered as submitted (i.e., "Did you really intend to order *twenty* copies or is this a typo for two?" or, "We entered an order for this title for you last week. Do you want a second copy, or is this an inadvertent duplicate?")? Do you have to remind your vendor of standard requests, such as number of invoice copies, the method of annual renewal, not to mix orders from other campus libraries, etc.? Will the vendor help you with back orders for runs or single issues? Will the vendor obtain quotes from publishers? Will the vendor request exceptions to publisher policy when you have a reasonable case? In general, do you supply the vendor with more information about changes and so on than the vendor supplies to you?

ADDITIONAL FACTORS

Another area to examine is the special services available from or provided by the vendor. Do you use the services that are offered and/or purchased? If you do not, you should either begin using the services or else negotiate a reduced service charge. (According to information discussed in the Tonkery and Merriman workshop at this conference, the "unbundling" of services and assessment of service charges based on actual library use is expected to occur soon.)

Many local factors influence the choice of a vendor or vendors, such as the level and type of automation employed by the library; the expertise of the serials acquisitions staff (including their foreign language facility); and the organizational implications of using multiple vendors.

A final point to consider in assessing vendor assignment is that all of these factors, pertaining to both library and vendor situations, will change over time. Many factors can affect vendor performance, such as automation enhancements, changes in publisher practices, expansions and/or retrenchments, and turnover among managerial and/or customer service personnel.

DECISION MAKING

Having carefully collected and considered all of this information, how do you decide whether to leave assignments as they are or to make changes? The central concern is to determine whether present service is effective and if pricing is reasonable. Obviously, trade-offs occur in which, for example, exceptional service may justify a higher service charge. Many choices are available, ranging from consolidation with fewer total vendors to splitting up present accounts and taking on boutique vendors to add more vendors overall.

Here are a few examples of situations in which boutique vendors can be effective. First, to support Ph.D. programs in the Romance languages, having a vendor located in each major country (Spain, Portugal, France and Italy) can be useful. A library with a strong East Asian collection might choose to use vendors in several Asian countries. If a library has a large Eastern European exchange program, using a vendor who will handle back run and single issue orders, plus subscriptions for titles not available on exchange, may be necessary. In general, it seems to me that vendors in the country of publication can provide better service. It seems to reflect human nature that a publisher would respond more positively to a claim from a fellow citizen than to one from a large international vendor. Finally, be aware that large vendors order from boutique vendors. If you have a large enough volume, you may save money and obtain better service by ordering directly from the boutique vendor.

To give you some less abstract information, I can describe vendor assignment at the two research libraries where I have worked. In one, over the course of several years, we shifted from using more than fifty vendors to using about fifteen, of which five were substantial accounts. In another library, we employ three large domestic/international vendors, two European/international vendors, one domestic standing order vendor, and ten to twelve boutique vendors. Many smaller libraries use two domestic and one foreign vendor.

You may decide to consolidate orders with vendors based on country of origin, specific publishers, and/or type of publication. To induce a vendor to handle a certain type of problem order, you may need to create a larger account by adding "standard" titles to the order mix.

Before committing orders to a new vendor, find out what expectations or requirements the vendor may have. Is there a minimum account size? Can you submit orders during six months or so to reach the minimum, or must all orders be sent at once? Will the vendor assign a single contact person to your account? How compatible are your procedures with those of the vendor? Identify services that you consider standard and make certain they are available.

PLANNING AND IMPLEMENTING VENDOR REASSIGNMENT

Once you have evaluated present service and decided what reassignments are desired, here are some suggestions for planning and implementing these decisions.

1. List the transfers to be made for several years. Begin with the most critical ones: titles presently with a vendor that is going out of business; orders that your present vendor will no longer handle; titles which must be reordered periodically since the publisher will not accept standing orders; lapsed orders, since

they may be with an inappropriate vendor; and orders that are placed directly with publishers without a good reason.
2. If orders are to be moved from one vendor to another, it is a courtesy to inform the old vendor before beginning the transfer. This is also a final opportunity to obtain the improvement in service not previously available.
3. With large transfers, plan to phase in over several years. Coordinating cancellations with summer renewal checklists is a time-saver because individual cancellation requests are unnecessary. Limit the amount to be transferred at one time. I suggest as a guideline no more than five to ten percent of total serials orders at one time, although local staffing levels may permit larger numbers.
4. Proceed with caution. Cancel early, obtain confirmation, and keep it on file permanently. Plan for gaps and overlaps in receipt. Negotiate the return for credit of duplicates and establish guidelines with the new vendor. Ask the new vendor to place your orders stating "formerly ordered through (previous vendor)." Even well-planned transfers generate problems, and their resolution is labor intensive.

NOTES

1. October Ivins, "Do Subscription Agents Earn Their Service Charges and How Can We Tell?" *Library Acquisitions: Practice and Theory*, in press.
2. Jan Derthick and Barbara B. Moran, "Serial Agent Selection in ARL Libraries," *Advances in Serials Management*, 1 (1986): 27.

ORGANIZATIONAL RESPONSES TO JOURNAL PRICING ISSUES: PLANS FOR ACTION

Serials Pricing Issues: News from the Field

Deana Astle

I would like to welcome all here this morning. As you are probably aware, this panel has undergone a metamorphosis since its inception, but I think you will be pleased with the result. We have two presenters whom I will introduce individually before they speak.

Well, here we are again, talking about the price of serials. A colleague expressed to me last fall that he hoped the pricing issue would be settled by this spring so that the profession could move on to something else. He was tired of hearing about prices, prices, prices. He was indulging in wishful thinking, but I am also convinced that he did not grasp the enormity of the impact which spiralling prices have had, and will continue to have, on the ability of

---

Deana Astle is Head of Technical Services, Clemson University, R. D. Cooper Library, Clemson, SC 29634-3001.

© 1990 by The Haworth Press, Inc. All rights reserved.

libraries to provide information to their users. The problem will not go away, especially if we choose to ignore it.

But has anything new been happening? Have we again been all talk and no action? Or have there been some serious attempts at networking? Have library organizations finally been getting involved? Are some publishers reaching out to librarians for serious input? Are models for measuring the relative worth of journals in a given discipline being developed? The answer to all of these questions is a resounding "Yes!"

We will hear in more detail about two of these developments, but I would like to take a few minutes to call your attention to other encouraging efforts. One of the most visible and successful attempts at networking for current awareness is the electronic newsletter edited by Marcia Tuttle of the University of North Carolina at Chapel Hill under the auspices of the American Library Association Resources and Technical Services Division Publisher/Vendor/Library Relations Committee's Task Force on Serial Pricing. I have a few copies printed from our mainframe that I will leave up here for people to examine. The newsletter includes such items as reports on meetings, bibliographies of relevant articles, notification of changes in the journal publishing industry, reports on egregious pricing, and other contributed commentaries. Through this and other means, information can be widely and quickly disseminated to a large body of interested readers rather than remaining the property of a small cadre of people. This newsletter is free. If you have a BITNET address, get in touch with Marcia to be put on the subscription list. It is also available on Faxon's DATALINX and EBSCO's EBSCONET. And, if you must, it is also available on paper through RTSD, although the printed newsletter is issued only every two months and is much less up to date than the electronic version.

Another example of networking is the newsletter produced by Katina Strauch at the College of Charleston. Called *Against the Grain* and available only in paper, it publishes information similar to that found in Marcia's newsletter, but also contains some longer articles. At present it is distributed primarily to the attendees of the College of Charleston Acquisitions Conference, although Katina is considering the possibility of wider distribution. The second issue, which will soon go to press, will be thirty pages long.

Some publishers are beginning to take librarians seriously and to seek their input. In April I was asked to speak to the annual meeting of the Publications Board of the American Institute of Physics so that the editors of the forty-plus journals published by AIP and its member societies could hear from one of their customers. Both the Executive Director and Director of Publications of AIP recognized the need to balance the expansionist desires of their editors against the realities of the library market, and wanted the editors to hear the realities from the horse's mouth, so to speak. My remarks on the "librarians' crises" were well received, and I learned that the AIP is considering establishing a library advisory council to give input to the Publications Board on a regular and continuing basis. This is encouraging, because the idea for my presentation and the proposed ongoing involvement of librarians came from the society itself.

Another effort from the publishing industry has been the sponsorship by the Society for Scholarly Publishing of two lively seminars on the future of the scholarly journal. The first was held in Chapel Hill, North Carolina, last October and the second this April in Lake Arrowhead, California. Publishers, librarians, academicians, vendors, and others discussed with considerable candor the present state of the journal, alternatives to the status quo including electronic journals, and future trends for this time-worn medium from the perspectives of the various constituencies. More information on these seminars is available in an article in the *Newsletter on Serials Pricing Issues*,[1] a recent article by Joe Hewett in *American Libraries*,[2] and from attendees at these meetings, many of whom are here today.

What are library organizations doing? The American Library Association has created a "blue ribbon" panel chaired by Robert Wedgeworth which is examining journal prices for RTSD. Called EALS (Economics of Access to Library Services), the panel has been holding open meetings at ALA for the past year and expects to be issuing a report in the not-too-distant future. As I see it, the significant feature of this panel is that it consists of representatives from such organizations as the Medical Library Association, the Special Libraries Association, the Canadian Library Association, the Library of Congress, the National Library of Medicine, the National Library of Canada, NASIG, ALA, and other interested groups. It is a consolidated effort of the profession to formulate a plan of action.

The Association of Research Libraries (ARL) decided last year that it was time for a serious examination of the pricing issue. ARL commissioned a study to test the conventional wisdom that some publishers, at least, are reaping considerable profits, and that subscription prices are rising much more rapidly than publishers' costs. An economics consulting firm was hired to do a statistical study of journal prices of four publishers—Pergamon Press, Elsevier, Springer-Verlag, and Plenum—from 1973 to 1987. The consulting firm constructed a publisher cost index and calculated price per page for each journal studied. Ann Okerson, our first presenter, who will be discussing the ARL report in some detail, was commissioned to write the background report to accompany this economic analysis, outlining the history and scope of the problem. This extensively annotated report looks in detail at the impact of rising prices on the budgets of ARL libraries and documents that these libraries have been able to purchase less and less of the serials universe even as expenditures for serials have soared.

Our second presenter, Dr. Paul Ribbe, a member of the geology faculty at Virginia Polytechnic Institute and a past president of the American Mineralogical Society, will be discussing the model he has created for measuring the relative worth of journals in a given discipline. It has great potential as a less subjective way to make judgments among journals as we perform our tasks as collection managers. His work is significant not only because he presents an interesting model, but also because the study has come from a scholar, writer, and editor, rather than from a librarian.

NOTES

1. Vicky Reich, "Society for Scholarly Publishing: Future of Scholarly Journals," *Newsletter on Serials Pricing Issues* no. 5 (May 28, 1989).

2. Joe A. Hewitt, "Altered States: Evolution or Revolution in Journal-Based Communications," *American Libraries* 6 (June 1989): 497-500.

Report on the ARL Serials Project

Ann Okerson

This final session returns to a favorite, recurring topic: serial prices. However, instead of talking about how expensive serials are, which we were doing at the first conference, and what some of the root causes are, which we were doing in the past couple of conferences, today we focus on solutions. Clearly, an understanding of causes is central to the evolution of answers, but the emphasis in the library community is shifting from describing the problems to finding resolution.

This morning I am to bring you up to date on what is, I believe, the most significant effort so far in evolving an action plan to combat high serials prices, the ARL Serials Initiative. After several discussions in the Association of Research Libraries' annual membership meetings and particularly in its Committee on Collection Development, the Association, in the spring of 1988, commissioned two external reports. The first was a study by Economic Consulting Services, Inc., of Washington, D.C. Its purpose was to analyze a sampling of price rises over time in Science/Technology/Medicine (STM) serial publications.

I was invited to write the second report to define the precise problem for the research library community, summarize the current debate, and propose a set of actions to resolve the problem. Although I have a full-time position, ECS has a backlog of contracting jobs, and the ARL staff have more than full-time jobs even without additional projects, we optimistically scheduled completion for fall 1988, all of us clearly underestimating the amount of time and ef-

---

Ann Okerson is Manager of Library Services, Jerry Alper, Inc., P.O. Box 218, Eastchester, NY 10707.

© 1990 by The Haworth Press, Inc. All rights reserved.

fort required for the work. The reports were finally handed in to ARL on March 31, 1989.

Let me describe the two commissioned studies, and if you have questions, please raise them in the discussion. Since the reports are just returning from printing, I assume that most of the NASIG audience has not had the opportunity to read them. They were mailed to all ARL directors in late April, prior to the May 9th membership meeting, but were embargoed until the Association had determined a course of action. Let me say at the outset that the focus of both reports is on the sciences and related disciplines.

THE ECS STUDY

ECS conducted an analysis of trends in average subscription prices and publication costs between the years 1973 and 1987. After several meetings, ARL staff and ECS decided that the analysis should focus on the four largest publishers of STM serials: Elsevier, Pergamon, Plenum, and Springer. The objective of the study was to test the hypothesis that subscription prices paid by U.S. libraries have risen at a more rapid rate than inflation in publishing costs. About 10 percent of the four publishers' titles were randomly selected as a sample. For its analysis, ECS requested annual subscription price and page counts. My role in this effort was to manage the title selection and data gathering project.

We did some trial runs for the data gathering process and were eventually able to hire three library assistants and one library school student to do a great deal of the work. We went into the stacks of about fifteen libraries to find the titles. My fondest memory is of the first serial I did, *Brain Research*. It took an entire Saturday morning in the closed stacks of the New York Academy of Medicine. I was in blue jeans, climbing chairs and ladders to reach volumes at ceiling level, just under the plumbing pipes. Some of the bindings were stuck together. It was very hot. To relieve tedium, the shelvers were playing rock and roll music on their radios. I was covered with dust and the floor was covered with my papers full of pencilled volume-by-volume page counts. The data gathering time averaged two hours per title, but *Brain Research* took twice that.

In its summary, the ECS analysis states that each targeted publisher has increased prices at a much faster rate than the rate at which costs have increased. In order to make these determinations, ECS first created a scholarly publisher cost model, which is described in their report. The range of difference between the annual growth rates of price per page and costs is from 2.6 to 6.7 percent. Restricting the analysis to the period 1980-87 increases the range from 4.5 to 12.9 percent. Over the period 1973-87, publisher profit ratios are estimated at between 40 and 137 percent.

THE OKERSON REPORT

This report consists of four chapters. The first, "Introduction and Background," describes the cyclical nature of the serials problem, which has been continuing at least throughout this century. Librarians' efforts to deal with the problem have waxed and waned depending on its severity and on the urgency of other demands and priorities. Chapter 1 also describes some other current activities underway and the origin of ARL interest in mounting a project.

The second chapter describes the effect of serial price increases on ARL libraries by examining the Association's annual statistics on overall expenditures, materials expenditures, serials expenditures, and growth in numbers of subscriptions. It compares ARL serials growth to growth in the serials "universe" as captured in the Ulrich's database, and cites price growth by discipline as shown in the ALA Library Materials Price Index Committee's annual indexes. Some specific library impacts are described, along with overall effects on the research community.

The effects on the library community have been severe. Particularly significant numbers from this chapter are that, between 1976 and 1988, the member libraries' average percent of expenditures devoted to serials rose from 40.4 percent to 56.2 percent of the materials budget. In the past three years, the average price of paid serials has risen by 32 percent to $115. The average price of serials from 1976 to 1988 rose by 350 percent, while the average holdings of ARL libraries dropped from 32 percent of the estimated serials universe to 26.4 percent.

Chapter 3, titled "Causes of the Serials Crisis," examines three alternative views of the problem.

1. As a consumer problem, discussing dual pricing, foreign exchange, privatization, concentration of publishers, growth in journal size, specialization of journals, and society versus commercial publishers' prices. The solutions call for librarians to become more vigilant consumers of high-priced materials rather than passive archivers of everything published.
2. As a systemic problem, describing the current publishing system as strained to its limits because of size, competitiveness, the academic tenure system, the academic grants system, historic expectations of libraries and faculty, and the profit-taking role of commercial publishers. The systemic problem requires significant changes on the part of all the participants in the chain in order to bring about solutions.
3. Finally, as an economic problem, describing academic serials as a "natural monopoly" product in which high fixed costs and low, inelastic demand lead to small circulations and high prices.

Possible solutions for the current crisis are implicit in the causes described, and Chapter 4 presents a summary and three recommendations. These recommendations (summarized below) address immediate consumer actions which should be taken, as well as root causes of the problem.

Recommendation 1: Immediate Actions

ARL should undertake a set of urgent actions to demonstrate the serious and immediate impact of the serials crisis. ARL should appoint a staff officer to lead its efforts with the university, government, and publishing communities.

Some of the actions enumerated under the first recommendation include research; development of subject-specific cost indexes for critical titles; programs of education and publicity directed not only toward librarians but also faculty, administrators, societies, and politicians; coordination of protest actions; consideration of resource-sharing and exploration of legal implications; review of quality of expensive titles; development of better understanding of journal usage patterns; and better internal bibliographic access to journal contents.

Recommendation 2:
The Role of Commercial Publishers

ARL should strongly advocate transfering the publication of research results from commercially issued serials to existing non-commercial channels. ARL should specifically encourage the creation of innovative non-profit alternatives to traditional commercial publishers.

This recommendation further suggests that the Association explore making publication through non-commercial channels the preferred means for reporting research results. It suggests that ARL support the development of inexpensive and not-for-profit alternatives to existing commercial journals.

In part, this recommendation is based on findings of various studies which are cited in Chapter 3, showing that the not-for-profit sector charges libraries per page or per character prices one-half to one-twentieth of those charged by comparable commercial publishers. This recommendation does not mean to imply that libraries must wage war on commercial publishers. It does say, however, that higher education, a not-for-profit enterprise, should seek closer alliances with societies and publishers who share similar aims. The recommendation does encourage libraries to support commercial publishers who are not high-priced and suggests that where commercial publishers can be more reasonable in their pricing, the library community will find their behavior acceptable. There is some discussion about replacing paper publishing with electronic means, but with the comment that at present this alternative is not well developed and shows no promise of being cheaper than paper.

Recommendation 3:
Quantity of Academic Publication

ARL should strongly advocate that university administrations and granting agencies change their policies for judging promotion, tenure, and funding, so as to minimize current pressures for excessive publication.

This recommendation suggests that ARL form a partnership with others in the scholarly community to find ways of managing the explosion in publishing, and that it apprise university administrators and granting agencies of the serious impact of current peer review practices on library budgets, collections, and mission. Current practices generate strong incentives to publish extensively. While the academic community must avoid impeding the flow of genuinely new results, much of the publishing explosion appears attributable to the current method of judging academic success through publication.

So far, I have largely quoted and paraphrased from the reports and their executive summaries. Let me enumerate briefly some things I learned during the course of this project that are not specifically stated in the reports, which I presented at the recent annual ARL membership meeting in Providence, Rhode Island.

1. The work done on serial prices to date represents a large, collective, and very impressive effort on the part of many individuals and institutions. The number of footnotes (by no means exhaustive) in the report, will attest to that. This work needs to continue, but it is time to learn new things, such as costs in non-science disciplines and comparative costs for new products such as those available on CD-ROM. We have to study journal quality. We have to improve serials price indexes. We would do well to go outside the library community for some of this work and commission new studies from faculty colleagues or graduate students doing research for dissertations.

2. In order to be successful, the energy put into the serials effort must be not only ambitious and collective but also coordinated. Until now, no single organization has assumed a coordinating role. ARL, with its manageable membership size and common goals, its interest in scholarly publishing, and its commitment to the preservation of the body of knowledge, is a logical organization to undertake such a function.

3. ARL is taken seriously by the scholarly community at large. It was gratifying that the mention of "Association of Research Libraries" was enough to get phone calls returned from scholarly society officers, foundations, academics, staff on Capitol Hill, and various related for-profit and not-for-profit organizations. It was even more gratifying to see how much interest and conversation the topics of serials quantity and serials prices generated, and how

many people wished to keep being informed and to be involved in next steps.

4. Finally, I had to conclude that one of the reasons librarians have not been more successful in dealing with problems of serial prices and proliferation is that most of us have not tried hard enough. If we are listened to, as we are, and if the community cares, as many do, it is time to adopt a new, active role within the academic community, no longer simply as intermediaries or water-bearers of academe, but as collaborators in the scholarly process.

Apparently, the membership of the Association agreed with both the reports and the above sentiments, because in an unprecedented action it almost unanimously accepted the recommendations and approved beginning a program in the next few weeks, volunteering an assessment for the serials initiative. As one director commented, "After all, it only means cancelling two Springer subscriptions."

Because the ARL stance is extraordinary, let me read you the text of resolutions and recommendations that were passed.

Resolutions

The members of the Association of Research Libraries (ARL) are concerned that rapidly escalating prices of scientific, technical and medical journals, especially those commercially published, have eroded their ability to serve the interests of the scholarly community. Reports to ARL . . . confirm that the research libraries of North America face an immediate economic crisis which translates into a crisis for the United States' and Canada's efforts at competing effectively in the world's research and development arena. The members and the Association are prepared to launch a multi-faceted program aimed at mobilizing the scholarly, scientific, academic communities and appropriate government bodies, to address this major issue.

It is the sense of the membership that the issue of serials pricing is of such a critical nature that we would support a supplementary dues assessment in order to expedite Association action.

—Adopted by ARL Membership, May 11, 1989

Recommendations for Further ARL Action

First, that ARL lead efforts with external constituencies to communicate the nature of the problem and the actions needed to address the causes of it as well as to develop several library-oriented consumer advocate services.

Second, that ARL orchestrate actions to introduce greater competition to the commercial publishers . . .

Third, that ARL form a partnership with scholarly groups to examine the scholarly publishing process and to find ways to understand the explosion in research and knowledge and to manage the concomitant explosion in publishing.

ARL should develop a program capability to direct these efforts. If necessary, unbudgeted 1989 funds may be expended to develop this capability.

— ARL Committee on Collection Development
and endorsed by the ARL Board, May 12, 1989

Board Actions

The Board of Directors acted on this mandate from membership, accepted the recommendations of the Collection Development Committee and authorized the following actions to be initiated by ARL staff:

- publicize the results of the studies;
- initiate contacts with scholarly and higher education groups;
- prepare options for establishing a serials prices program capability at ARL;
- expend unbudgeted 1989 funds, if necessary, to advance the recommendations.

—Adopted by the ARL Board, May 12, 1989

Last week, the Association received statements of support on its recommendations from leaders of the Association of American Universities, the American Council of Learned Societies, and the

American Association for the Advancement of Science, which is preparing an editorial for its journal, *Science*.

With the approval of these reports by its membership, ARL has successfully completed Phase I and begun Phase II of its agenda, which involves preparing a more detailed plan of action and identifying associated costs for presentation to the July 1989 ARL Board. If that plan is approved, specific activities should begin in late summer. As of their last meeting, ARL staff thinking is that the Association's role in scholarly publishing and serials costs will proceed on three different fronts—sciences, social sciences, and the humanities—since the associated needs and problems vary greatly. While the profession knows something about journal prices in STM, we know very little about the other disciplines.

I urge you all to read the ARL serials reports and preferably to get your library to buy at least one copy, so that the Association can recover costs and use the funds towards further work. The Association and library community particularly request your support and your ideas as future activities go forward. You may request free copies of the Summary and Overview by sending a self-addressed, stamped envelope to ARL, 1527 New Hampshire Avenue, N.W., Washington, D.C., 20036. The reports are also available from ARL at a cost of $20 to members and $60 to non-members.

BIBLIOGRAPHY

The following reports were funded through a special assessment of the Association of Research Libraries membership and a grant form the Council on Library Resources.

Economic Consulting Services, Inc. *A Study of Trends in Average Prices and Costs of Certain Serials Over Time*. Washington, D.C.: Economic Consulting Services, Inc., March 31, 1989.

Okerson, Ann. *Of Making Many Books There Is No End: Report on Serial Prices for the Association of Research Libraries*. Eastchester, N.Y., April 1989.

A Scientist's Assessment of a Microcosm of the Serials Universe

Paul H. Ribbe

In their endless pursuit of prestige[1] in a "publish or perish" environment, academic researchers are rarely inclined to investigate objectively the journals to which they submit the fruit of their labors. In any discipline or subset thereof, there are subjective perceptions of what journals are "the best," "the fastest," "the easiest," "the cheapest," and which must be read or may safely be ignored. But which journals are truly outstanding? That is, which are widely circulated, read, and quoted? And which are not? Furthermore, in the climate of crisis created by spiralling costs of serials, which give best (or least) value for the money? Is it possible to find criteria that will help serials librarians—and the academic colleagues they serve—judge which journals ought to be cancelled, or better yet, help convince researchers themselves to shun such journals?

These questions were raised in my 1987 presidential address to the Mineralogical Society of America (MSA).[2] In "Mammon and Prestige in Mineralogy and Petrology," I reported the results of an investigation of the distribution of federal funding for research among U.S. earth science departments[3] and a study of the tribunal in which the prestige of research is ostensibly judged, namely the serials literature.[4,5] The latter was an intensive look at a small sample of kindred journals that represent mineralogy-related disciplines of earth science. In this paper I have updated, expanded and revised

---

Paul H. Ribbe is Series Editor of *Reviews in Mineralogy* and Professor of Mineralogy at the Department of Geological Sciences, Virginia Polytechnic Institute and State University, Blacksburg, VA 24061.

The author wishes to thank Marianne Stern for her faithful assistance in gathering data for this version of his study.

my assessment of these journals. I offer it as a possible model for judging, in the context of cost, the relative quality of scientific serials in general.

JOURNALS ASSESSED

Because English is the language of approximately 88 percent of the half-million articles and approximately 96 percent of the 7.5 million citations listed in the 1986 *Science Citation Index*,[6] I chose a limited number of primarily English-language journals to represent the research disciplines in which MSA members participate, namely, mineralogy (including crystallography), petrology, and geochemistry.[7] The list in Table 1 contains both commercial and not-for-profit journals and a few published commercially under contract to professional societies.

TOOLS OF ASSESSMENT

Possible measures of relative reputations of the selected journals include:

1. bibliometric rankings that are reported annually in *Journal Citation Reports* volumes of the *Science Citation Index*;
2. circulation data related to numbers of institutional subscribers and of individual members of professional societies;
3. information in the "Acknowledgments" section of an article about the source or sources of financial support for the research reported therein. This provides a link to another measure of prestige, i.e., funding obtained by authors on a competitive basis.

Science Citation Index (SCI)

Of particular relevance in any evaluation of scientific journals are the *SCI Journal Citation Reports* (JCR) that answer these basic questions: "How often has a journal been cited? What journals have cited it? How frequently . . .? What journals has it cited? How often? What are the chronological patterns of citation (older or

TABLE 1. Mineralogy-related journals and their publishers listed alphabetically. Those in italics were investigated bibliometrically on a limited scale.

Journal Title	Abbreviation	Publisher(s)
American Journal of Science	A J S	Kline Geology Laboratory, Yale University
American Mineralogist	Am Min	Mineralogical Society of America
Bulletin de Minéralogie	Bull Min	Societé francaise de Minéralogie et de Cristallographie
Canadian Mineralogist	Can Min	Mineralogical Association of Canada
Chemical Geology	Ch G	Elsevier Science Publishers B.V.
Clay Minerals	Cl Min	Clay Minerals Group, Mineralogical Society of Great Britain; Blackwell Scientific Publications
Clays and Clay Minerals	Cl & Cl Min	Clay Minerals Society
Contributions to Mineralogy and Petrology	C M P	Springer-Verlag GmbH
Earth and Planetary Science Letters	*E P S L*	*Elsevier Science Publishers B.V.*
Economic Geology	*Ec Geol*	*Economic Geology Publishing Co.*
Geochemical Journal	G'chem J	Geochemical Society of Japan
Geochimica et Cosmochimica Acta	G C A	Geochemical Society and Meteoritical Society; Pergamon Press
Journal of Metamorphic Geology	J M G	Blackwell Scientific Publications
Journal of Petrology	J Pet	Oxford University Press
Lithos	Lithos	Universitetsforlaget (through 1983); Elsevier Scientific Publishers B.V.
Mineralium Deposita	Min Dep	Springer-Verlag GmbH; Society of Geology Applied to Mineral Deposits
Mineralogical Magazine	Min Mag	Mineralogical Society of Great Britain
Mineralogy and Petrology [*formerly* Tschermaks mineralogische und petrographische Mitteilungen]	Min & Pet [TMPM]	Österreichischen Mineralogischen Gesellschaft; Springer-Verlag GmbH
Physics and Chemistry of Minerals	P C M	Springer-Verlag GmbH
Reviews in Mineralogy	*RiM*	*Mineralogical Society of America*

newer material)? What is the degree of self-citation?"[8] I collected data on the journals in Table 1 for the years 1980-1987 from the JCR volumes in the eight SCI annual series. Each of these volumes contains an updated reference list of recent and the more important older studies involving citation analysis applied to a variety of disciplines.[9] Each also gives definitions and caveats regarding the various bibliometric parameters chosen for use in this study. They are:

Impact Factor

Impact factor is basically a ratio between citations and citable source items published. For example, if the hypothetical *Journal of Minpet* (JM) contained 32 articles in 1985 and 28 in 1986, and JM was referenced in all journals (including itself) 65 times in 1985 and 55 times in 1986, the impact factor reported in 1987 would be (65 + 55)/(32 + 28) = 120/60 = 2.000. The 65 citations in 1985 include references to any articles in any issue of JM from its beginning through 1985; likewise 1986. Nearly all earth science journals have impact factors of 4.0 or less. "The impact factor is useful in evaluating the significance of absolute citation frequencies," tending ". . . to discount the advantage of large journals over small ones," and of frequently issued and older journals over less frequently issued and new ones. The impact factor permits "some qualification of quantitative data"; it is ". . . algorithmic and objective, but nonetheless useful . . ."[10] In Figure 1a are plotted the total numbers of citations to a serial (for all years of its existence) divided by the number of source items in the period 1984-1987 versus the mean impact factor for the same period. The trend is predictable. A notable exception on the high side is the *American Journal of Science* (AJS), a 170-year-old serial whose editors have insisted on publishing only carefully reviewed, major papers of broad interest to the profession; on the low side are *Physics and Chemistry of Minerals* (PCM), which in 1987 doubled its usual number of papers, and *Reviews in Mineralogy* (RiM), a series of graduate-level text and reference books, published at the rate of one or two a year and thus not a serial of the usual sort.

Immediacy Index

This is "a measure of how quickly the 'average article' in a particular journal is cited."[11] For example, the immediacy index of JM for 1986 is calculated by dividing the number of all journals' 1986 citations of articles in the 1986 JM by the total number of articles in JM in 1986. Articles published earlier in the year are more likely to

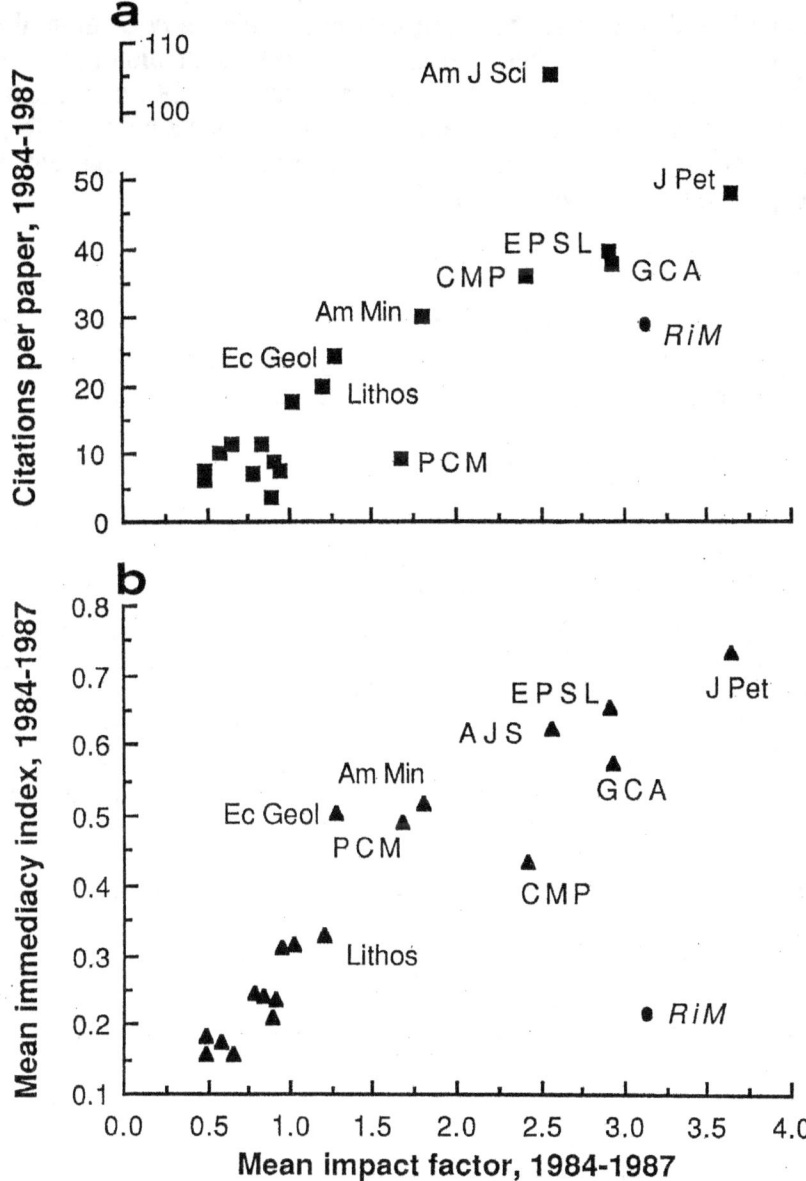

FIGURE 1. (a) The total number of citations of a journal divided by its total number of source items for the years 1984-87. (b) Immediacy index vs. impact factor, both averaged over the four-year period 1984-87. Data are in Table 2. Abbreviations represent names of the "more prestigious" journals (see Table 1).

be cited, and of course those journals issued biweekly or monthly are likely to have higher immediacy indexes than bimonthly or quarterly publications. A plot of four-year mean values versus mean impact factors for the same years (Figure 1b) shows a high positive correlation, so I have chosen to rely on impact factor alone when comparing the prestige of journals.

Citing Half-Life and Self-Citation Rate

These parameters were not taken into account in assessing the prestige of mineralogy, petrology and geochemistry journals, but see the citation study of earth science journals by Garfield.[12]

Sources of Financial Support

The total dollar awards of NSF's Division of Earth Sciences to the 82 institutions (ranked according to "scholarly quality" by a National Council of Education survey[13]) almost exactly parallels the average number of published papers from those institutions (see Figure 2a,b). This comes as no surprise, but it led me to test the following hypothesis: the more prestigious journals report the more prestigious research which in turn is more heavily supported-not only by larger amounts of money but also by larger numbers of grants-than research of "less importance." Thus, for the journals in Table 1 (those not in italics), we perused the "Acknowledgments" section of every article that had at least one author who gave an address in the United States. Our purpose was to determine the source, or lack thereof, of financial support for the research reported in each paper. In order to limit the bookkeeping, only federally funded sources were counted for most journals. The Petroleum Research Fund (PRF) of the American Chemical Society was specifically included for two of the journals.

Data were collected from 4,223 papers with 8,818 U.S. authors (38 percent and 35 percent of the respective total numbers of papers and authors in the seventeen journals for the period 1980-88, see Table 2 for summary; details are available from the author upon request). The dominant federal granting agencies are the National Science Foundation (NSF), the Department of Energy (DOE) and the National Aeronautics and Space Administration (NASA).

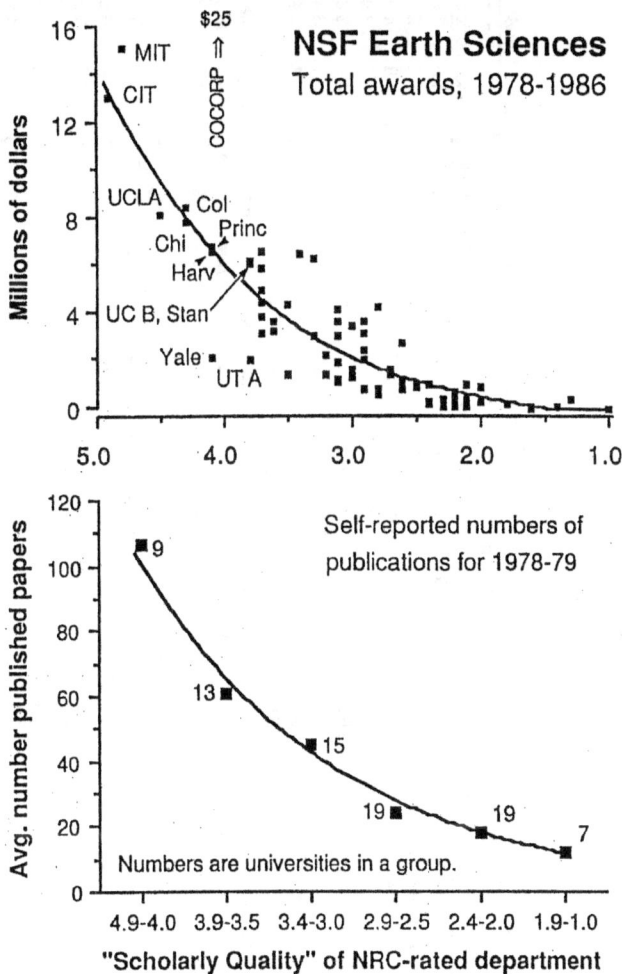

FIGURE 2. (a) Grand totals of amounts awarded by the National Science Foundation Earth Sciences Division to the 82 institutions rated according to "scholarly quality" for the period 1978-86. (b) The average number of publications per institution (self-reported for 1978-79) as a function of "scholarly quality."[14]

Strictly speaking, the North Atlantic Treaty Organization (NATO) is not a U.S. federal agency. Furthermore, its support of scientific research is usually limited to travel and per diem expenses in connection with international collaboration; thus, it does not rank with

TABLE 2

Journal name (Table 1)	Totals for 1980-88 (obs'd)				Means, 1984-87 (JCR)				Price information			Cost/ quality index	Percent grant support 1980-88						
	Number of...		Papers with US authors	Number of US authors	Cita-tions	Impact factor	Source items	Immed. index	1988 price	1988 US $ price/ paper	Price in '80 $		NSF	DOE	NASA	NATO	Fed'l agency	Unsup-ported	PRF
	Papers	Authors																	
AJS	249	515	201	399	3803	2.563	36	0.623	80	2.35	1.61	0.92	56	5	3	0	15	19	n.d.
Am Min	1278	2884	892	1741	4397	1.798	146	0.517	140	0.89	0.61	0.50	51	4	6	1	20	20	n.d.
Bull Min	641	1538	41	65	450	0.789	64	0.246	120	2.11	1.44	2.67	28	3	0	3	18	49	n.d.
Can Min	602	1422	161	335	786	0.834	73	0.241	56	0.75	0.51	0.90	34	2	3	2	29	30	n.d.
Chem G	993	2323	221	457	1201	0.944	166	0.313	1000	n.a.	n.a.	n.a.	30	9	4	0	25	33	n.d.
Cl Min	426	1043	25	43	468	0.918	55	0.237	135	3.21	2.20	3.50	21	6	0	6	3	64	n.d.
Cl&Cl Min	628	1498	302	657	1175	1.027	68	0.317	96	1.23	0.84	1.20	25	5	2	0	17	46	6
CMP	1196	2666	488	963	4917	2.420	136	0.434	1363	10.48	7.19	4.33	62	3	7	1	8	19	n.d.
EPSL	n.a.	n.a.	n.a.	n.a.	7591	2.909	192	0.65	707	n.a.	n.a.	n.a.	n.a.	n.a.	n.a.	n.a.	n.a.	n.a.	n.a.
Ec Geol	n.a.	n.a.	n.a.	n.a.	3020	1.270	124	0.5	80	0.63	0.43	0.50	n.a.	n.a.	n.a.	n.a.	n.a.	n.a.	n.a.
GCA	2059	5263	1357	3164	9220	2.920	244	0.575	375	1.35	0.92	0.46	39	11	19	0	16	13	3
G'Chem J	289	671	40	93	312	0.581	36	0.174	166	n.a.	n.a.	n.a.	36	2	4	0	13	45	n.d.
JMG	165	324	26	44	92	0.897	26	0.210	170	4.36	2.99	4.86	71	3	0	7	7	12	n.d.
J Pet	295	614	118	199	1860	3.644	39	0.735	180	4.29	2.94	1.18	66	4	7	1	9	14	n.d.
Lithos	243	509	34	62	488	1.202	24	0.329	157	4.76	3.26	3.96	26	2	2	2	9	59	n.d.
Min&Pet	255	534	18	26	160	0.496	25	0.183	320	7.62	5.22	15.38	32	0	0	9	37	22	n.d.
Min Dep	342	698	23	35	297	0.498	39	0.159	188	5.08	3.48	10.21	10	3	10	10	16	52	n.d.
Min Mag	816	1607	90	165	1008	0.658	88	0.158	195	2.29	1.57	3.49	27	3	2	0	33	32	n.d.
PCM	539	1325	186	370	618	1.677	66	0.492	515	5.92	4.06	3.53	60	7	3	5	13	13	n.d.
RiM	n.a.	n.a.	n.a.	n.a.	405	3.103	14	0.28	**	**	**	n.a.	n.a.	n.a.	n.a.	n.a.	n.a.	n.a.	n.a.

n.a. = not available or not applicable; n.d. - not determined; ** RiM is free to Am Min subscribers.

NSF, DOE or NASA in terms of the amount of money contributed to a research effort. But because acknowledgments of NATO grants were recorded in the initial study, they are reported in Table 2 with the others.

If the U.S. author(s) of a paper acknowledged financial support of one or more grants from one or more agencies, all grants were recorded. If one or more of the authors gave a federal agency (such as the U.S. Geological Survey, U.S. Bureau of Mines, Smithsonian Institution, Brookhaven National Laboratory [NL], Oak Ridge NL, Los Alamos NL, etc.) as an address, it was assumed that his or her work was "supported" by a federal agency. Each author with such an address would be recorded in the "Fed'l agency" column, and any grants or contracts they might have acknowledged were also counted.

In order to normalize the data to account for multiple grants and multiple federally employed authors, I counted the percent of "unsupported" papers straightforwardly, i.e., by dividing their number by the total number of papers with U.S. authors. Values in the column "Percent grant support, 1980-88 . . . NSF," for example, were calculated by dividing the number of papers referencing one or more NSF grants by the total number of papers referencing (NSF + DOE + NASA + NATO + Fed'l), and then, in order to normalize that number to account for the fact that more than one funding or federal agency might have supported a single article, this quotient was multiplied by the percent of supported papers [= (100 – "% unsupported")].

"Unsupported" Research Papers

Nearly every professional paper is written by someone whose salary is paid by someone else and who is provided with a place in which to work. Thus the concept of "unsupported" research is mythical in the absolute sense. But in the context of this study, characterizing an article as "unsupported" indicates that no acknowledgment was specifically given to NSF, DOE, NASA or NATO (or PRF), nor was an author's address an agency of the federal government or a national laboratory.

To get an idea of to what extent "unsupported" research papers by U.S. authors are actually unsupported, I examined the acknowledgments of 139 such articles in the *American Mineralogist* (1980-86) and found that 60 percent had absolutely no references to financial support. The other 40 percent could be apportioned about equally among (1) authors with industrial addresses, (2) those at the Carnegie Institution's Geophysical Laboratory, (3) those who acknowledged small external grants (Sigma Xi, Geological Society of America, etc.), and (4) others with (probably small) internal grants from university research foundations.

ASSESSMENT OF PRESTIGE

Impact Factor and Support of Research

Funded Research

The agencies supporting the research reported in our selection of journals are dominated by NSF, NASA and DOE, in that order. In fact, of all papers by U.S. authors that are supported by the big three granting agencies, about 75 percent are funded by NSF—most of these by the Earth Science Division, followed distantly by Ocean Sciences and the Materials Research Division.

Figure 3a summarizes data from Table 2 and shows the relationship between the percent of papers by U.S. authors supported by the three primary granting agencies (for 1980-88) as a function of the mean impact factors of the journals. Clearly, the "better" journals (impact factors greater than 1.5) are attracting by far the greater percentages of funded research papers.

"Unsupported" Research

An examination of the percentages of papers by U.S. authors that contain no reference to a federal laboratory, museum or granting agency, or to PRF or NATO, indicates that the better journals average approximately 16 percent "unsupported" papers, and those with impact factor less than 1.5 average around 40 percent "unsupported" papers.[16]

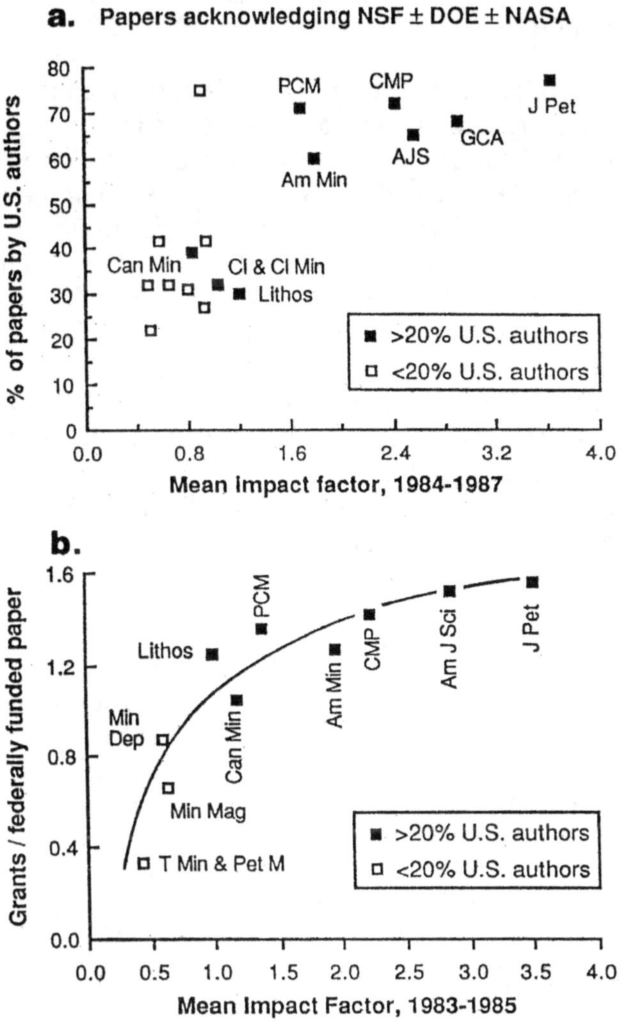

FIGURE 3. (a) Mean impact factors of journals for the years 1984-87 plotted against percentages of papers by U.S. authors who acknowledged research support from NSF, NASA, and DOE in the years 1980-88. (b) Average number of federal grants per paper, as acknowledged by U.S. authors in papers considered to be "supported" (see text), plotted against mean impact factor (1983-85) for eleven journals.[15]

Multiple Grants

Although dollar amounts of grants were never mentioned in journal articles, many U.S. authors acknowledged multiple grants from one or more federal agencies, including those implicit in their addresses. Such data were gathered from only eleven of the seventeen journals (Table 2). They are presented in Figure 3b as a plot of average number of grants per federally funded paper, where "federally funded paper" includes not only those containing acknowledged grants but also those whose authors list addresses at government agencies. Papers by federal employees are not funded by NSF, and generally not by NASA or DOE, although there are occasional exceptions for NASA and many more so for DOE, which heavily supports research at some of the national laboratories. Not surprisingly, the curves in Figures 3a and 3b have the same general form. Grants beget more grants.[17]

Circulation

The circulation of a particular journal is generally not a reliable measure of the esteem in which it is held by the scientific community. A commercial journal is not likely to be subscribed to by individual scientists unless the journal is also sponsored, edited or otherwise negotiated by a not-for-profit professional society and made available to its membership at a price considerably below institutional subscription rates (*Geochimica et Cosmochimica Acta* is a notable example). Most societies publish and market their own journals privately, and lacking the profit motive, they often are constrained to subsidize the publication costs with volunteer editorial labor (commercial publishers do the same) and voluntary or even mandatory page charges and/or charges to the authors for reprints. So price is not unrelated to circulation, but as discussed below, price is likely to become a major issue in the effectiveness or even the survival of some journals.

Very few scientists have any idea of the relative circulation of the periodicals to which they submit their research papers. And until recently, few of them have given any thought to how much that journal is costing their library. My conversations on this subject with certain prominent members of the community of mineralogists and petrologists have been revealing: most simply are interested in fast publication (preferably with a minimum of hassle from reviewers), with no page charges and free reprints. Some occasionally publish in journals outside their traditional areas of endeavor, but most are concerned with communicating as rapidly as possible within their "invisible colleges."[18] As indicated above in the study of impact factor and financial support of research, few scientists of repute are likely to sacrifice much in the way of perceived prestige of the journal they choose in order to obtain quick, "cheap" publication, but almost none have given any thought to circulation or price — they would assume that the best institutions subscribe to every journal regardless of price. This may not be a valid assumption in the future.

Figure 4 is a plot of circulation data collected almost entirely through personal communication with journal editors, secretaries of societies, and employees of various status within commercial pub-

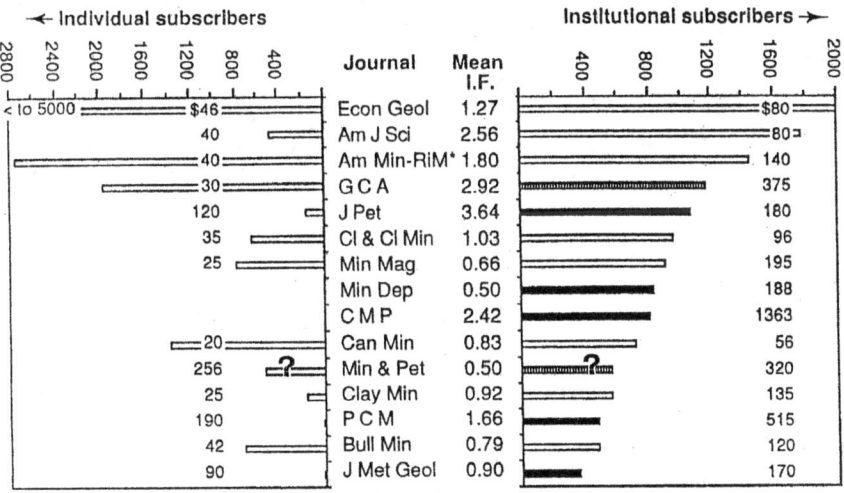

FIGURE 4. Circulation data for fourteen journals divided between individual subscribers (left) and institutional subscribers (right). *The institutional subscription rate for *American Mineralogist* (Am Min) includes *Reviews in Mineralogy* (RiM, which has an impact factor of 3.10). Question marks on *Mineralogy and Petrology* (Min & Pet) data indicate uncertainty as to the distribution of total circulation of 710 volumes between individual and institutional subscribers. Prices are for 1988 and impact factors are averages for 1984-87.[19]

lishing establishments (except Elsevier Scientific Publishers, who declined to release figures). In the bar graph to the left are plotted the numbers of individual subscribers. Prices listed there are the 1988 dues paid to professional societies, or (in the case of *American Journal of Science and Economic Geology*) to a nonprofit publisher, or in the case of *Physics and Chemistry of Minerals* and *Journal of Metamorphic Petrology* to MSA as a special reduced price from the publishers. Note that significant numbers of individuals choose to subscribe only to journals of professional societies whose prices are low. Exceptions are the *American Journal of Science* and the *Journal of Petrology*, whose reputations are outstanding and whose prices to individuals for personal use are moderate.

In the graph on the right are plotted the numbers of institutional subscribers who pay the 1988 rates recorded on the bars. Open bars represent journals of professional societies (average price of eight: $113), shaded bars represent journals of societies that are published and marketed by commercial scientific presses (average price of two: $347), and black bars represent commercial for-profit journals (average price of the five shown: $483; if the two Elsevier publications are added, the average price is $481). The highest priced journal is *Contributions to Mineralogy and Petrology*, which at $1,363 for 1988 cost only $235 less than the total price of all *ten* journals published by professional societies; it should gross nearly $1.1 million at its 1987 circulation rate.

"Twigging" is practiced among commercial publishers looking for new markets and ways to serve the scientific community; it involves introducing new journals that represent ever-more-specialized subdisciplines. The only recent "twig" in our list is Blackwell's *Journal of Metamorphic Geology*, whose appearance in 1983, just before the dramatic upturn of European currencies relative to the U.S. dollar, may account for its very low circulation of 364 copies in 1987. To be sure, Bowker[20] recently said that "we [Blackwell Scientific Publications, Ltd.] are very conscious of the need to avoid 'twigging' of journals, and indeed we are moving cautiously in the opposite direction by encouraging mergers of existing titles." Unfortunately, merging is likely to occur only among journals published by a single company and probably only when profitability is threatened or additional profitability is promised.

The two mineralogy-petrology journals with highest prices per article have similar titles and meet the first criterion for potential merger—but probably not the second. Commendably, in 1988 three mineralogical societies in continental Europe (West Germany, France, and Italy) combined their separate journals into one, called the *European Journal of Mineralogy*.

In the assessment of prestige, circulation is obviously of minor importance. However, in an author's choice of a journal, it may well be of some relevance, now that it is known for at least these few publications. Although in the past many authors have had little concern for anything other than their own interests in the choice of a journal, the price of journals to libraries has recently emerged as a significant factor to be taken into consideration.

ASSESSMENT OF PRICES

The rapidly rising costs of serials has been the major preoccupation of librarians and library committees of academic faculty for the last few years. The problem was exacerbated by a declining dollar in foreign currency markets that only recently is making a comeback (see Figure 5), which is supposedly good for libraries but bad for the U.S. economy.

In order to meaningfully compare the prices of journals, it is necessary to normalize the database in some manner. To consider price per page would be misleading, because formats vary widely. So in Figure 6 I have chosen to plot price per source item (as defined by the *Science Citation Index*) for the years 1980-88. It is obvious from a cursory glance at Figure 6 that serials published by professional societies (*Geochimica et Cosmochimica Acta, American Mineralogist, Mineralogical Magazine*; lower right) have much lower prices per source item to libraries than commercial journals. These were chosen to be representative-*Canadian Mineralogist, Economic Geology* and *Clays and Clay Minerals* are priced similarly to *American Mineralogist*, and *Bulletin de Minéralogie*; *American Journal of Science*, and *Geochemical Journal* have prices like *Mineralogical Magazine* and *Geochimica et Cosmo-chimica Acta* (GCA). There has tended to be little fluctuation in these prices, especially in inflation-adjusted dollars, but note that the price of

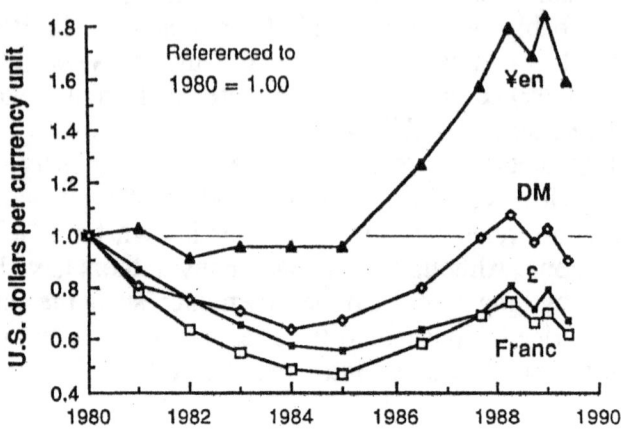

FIGURE 5. Values of Japanese ¥en, West German deutsche Mark (DM), British pound (£) and French franc, normalized to their U.S. dollar equivalents in 1980. The relative value of the Dutch florin almost exactly mimics that of the German Mark. Data from *Statistical Abstracts, The Washington Post* and *The Wall Street Journal*.

GCA increased by 25 percent in 1989 as the result of a new contract that was negotiated between the Geochemical Society and Pergamon.

Our sample of commercial for-profit journals (all foreign) certainly reflects fluctuations in exchange rates (compare Figures 5 and 6). But prices to libraries started relatively high and some have risen precipitously in recent years. For example, with 130 citable articles in 1988, Springer-Verlag's *Contributions to Mineralogy and Petrology* cost $10.48 per source item, an increase of 75 percent in inflation-adjusted dollars over already high 1980 prices. *Mineralogy and Petrology*, another Springer-Verlag journal, was the most expensive of all in 1980, but in inflation-adjusted dollars it registered no increase through 1988. The cost of *Lithos* took a big jump in 1985, a year after its publication was assumed by Elsevier. The prices per source item of commercial serials range from more than sixteen times as expensive as *Economic Geology* to as low as three

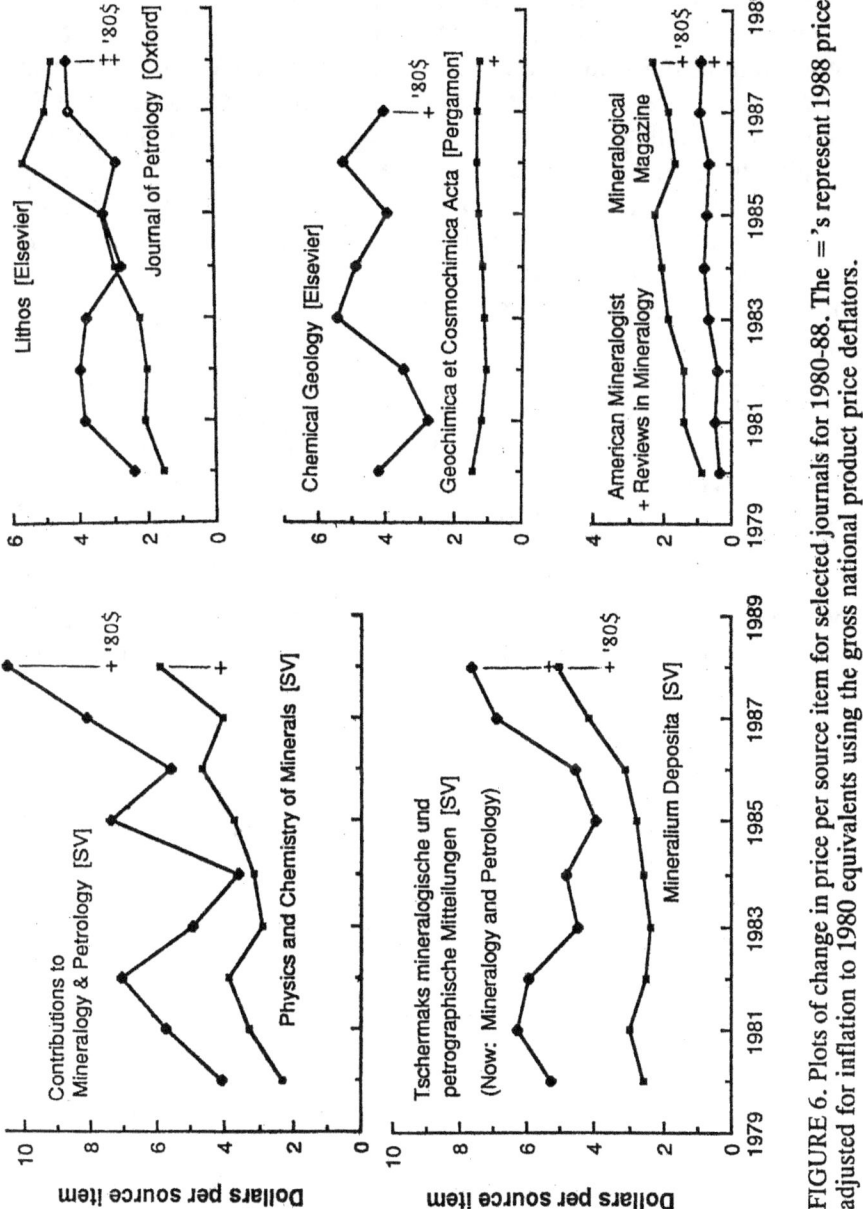

FIGURE 6. Plots of change in price per source item for selected journals for 1980–88. The =='s represent 1988 prices adjusted for inflation to 1980 equivalents using the gross national product price deflators.

times as expensive as the European mineralogical society journals, judging by their North American (U.S. dollar) prices.

Discriminatory pricing is commonly practiced by commercial publishers in both directions across the Atlantic Ocean. Seventeen commercial presses in England averaged 68 percent surcharges to North American subscribers in a recent year, surcharges most often totally unexplained or otherwise justified as "mailing and handling costs." In fact, mail rates to Europe from the United States are only $0.22 per issue more than domestic rates for the *American Mineralogist* (approximately 17 ounces per issue in 1988), and unless the International Postal Union is allowing extraordinarily lopsided pricing, this excuse for surcharges is hollow.

Recently I expressed dismay at discovering discriminatory pricing by MSA's sister organization, the not-for-profit Mineralogical Society of Great Britian (MSGB).[21] In their three journals they advertise prices both in pounds sterling and U.S. dollars. The latter have been very much higher than the former in the period 1980-88 (see Figure 7), amounting to a total of $955.85. My indignation met with reproof and an explanation that all during this time it had been possible to pay *either* the sterling price *or* the dollar price. I called the subcription agency which handles a very large proportion of

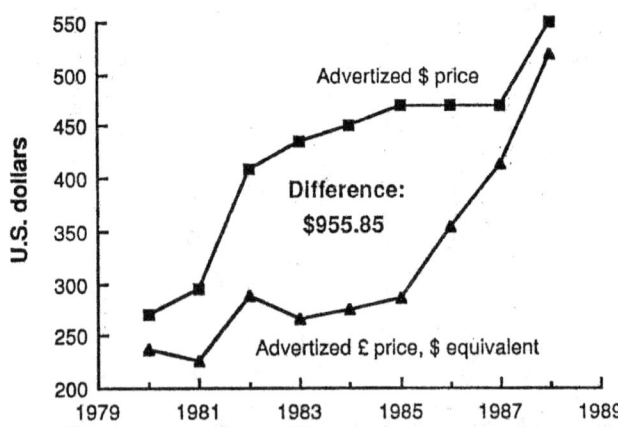

FIGURE 7. For the three journals managed by the Mineralogical Society of Great Britain (*Mineralogical Magazine, Mineralogical Abstracts* and *Clay Minerals*), the U.S. dollar equivalent values of the advertised sterling price are compared with the advertised U.S. dollar price. Difference for the nine years is $955.85.

U.S. library subscriptions to MSGB journals, and they confirmed that they indeed had been invoiced on an either/or basis but had always paid the dollar price! This, they assured me, will change. Meanwhile MSGB has enjoyed a windfall amounting to $350,000± in the past nine years, the termination of which will have fiduciary implications for subscribers and members alike.

By contrast, the advertised U.S. dollar prices of *Physics and Chemistry of Minerals* (Springer-Verlag) were less than 5 percent higher than the German currency prices between 1980 and 1987. Elsevier sells its journals only in the currency of the country in which it is printed (a practice I applaud), so apart from that portion of the price which is pure profit, both publisher and purchaser are at the mercy of the foreign exchange merchants, win or lose.

CONCLUSIONS

It is somewhat arbitrary to consider journals purely in monetary terms, although in times of austerity "cost per source item" is a reasonable point of reference. Collective bargaining with the commercial press is being considered, but unfortunately for most libraries, cancellation may be the only recourse because restraint-of-trade laws preclude certain types of collective actions (such as boycotts). Of course it is naive to think that a significant number of cancellations will force journal prices down: publishers' pricing is calculated on a unit basis, and prices will inevitably rise to those still well endowed enough to continue all their subscriptions. But this cannot go on indefinitely. "There is a widespread belief that many small-circulation journals will go out of business."[22] Market pressures will prevail.

But the literature of science is not simply a matter of economics. If it were, we would cancel a few highly priced journals and continue subscribing to the many reasonably priced ones. Journal quality is a paramount consideration, and factoring quality into price is an interesting exercise.[23] Figure 8 is a crude effort to do just that. On the left ordinate axis is plotted the 1988 price per source item for sixteen journals. It is noteworthy that only commercial journals have prices in excess of $3.25 per article, reaching a high of $10.48.

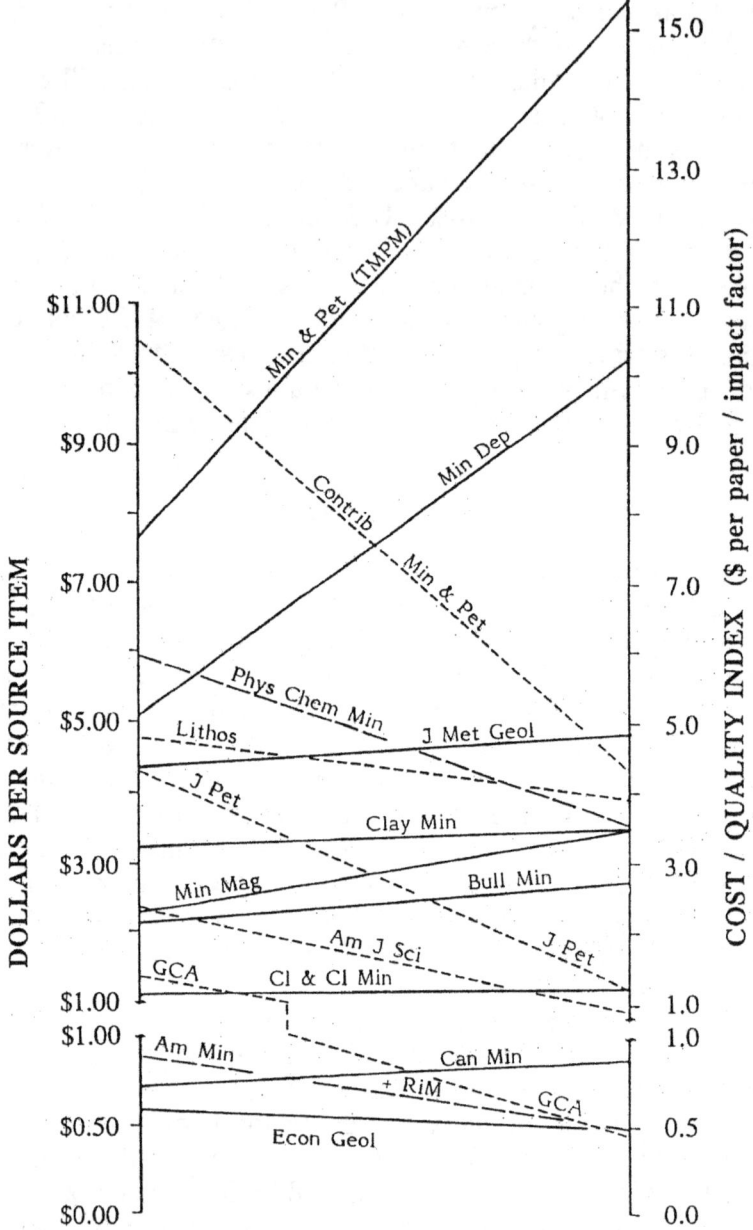

FIGURE 8. 1988 prices in current dollars per source item (left) compared to the "cost/quality index" (right), which is determined by dividing the same prices by the journal's mean impact factor for 1984-87. The lower portion of the scale (0.0-1.0) is expanded by a factor of 2.5. Note that the one university journal (Am J Sci) and all professional society journals have prices of less than $3.25 per source item.

On the right ordinate of Figure 8 are points calculated by dividing the prices per source item by the mean impact factor assigned to the journal by SCI JCR for the years 1984-87 (Table 2). The line joining the data points for a particular journal will have a positive slope if the impact factor (I.F.) is greater than 1.00 and a negative slope if I.F. is less than 1.00. Note, however, that a low-priced journal (*American Mineralogist*; I.F. = 1.8, not including *Reviews in Mineralogy*), with an impact factor nearly the same as a high-priced journal (*Contributions to Mineralogy and Petrology*; I.F. = 2.4), has a much lower negative slope than its counterpart.

How best to use such a compilation is open to debate. A library committee might decide that lines with high positive slopes, representing as they do both a high price and a low impact factor, would implicate those journals for cancellation. Alternatively, it might choose a reference point on the right axis of (say) 4.0 or 5.0, above which similar judgments would be rendered. Whether an individual author submitting a paper for publication will take these data into consideration or not is complicated by personal needs for prestige, fast publication, free reprints, and/or assured circulation to members of the "invisible college."

It is clear that university administrations, departments and funding agencies should be urged to de-emphasize the quantity of publications that a faculty member must produce to stay competitive, thereby counteracting the trend to fragmentation and "shingling" of research reports. It is also incumbent upon library committees to educate authors in a variety of disciplines to the cost/quality idea so that they will join the fray to contain or perhaps even reverse the cost and proliferation of serials.

NOTES

1. Pres-tige (prê-stēzh') "1. An illusion; a conjuring trick; a deception; an imposture." *Oxford English Dictionary*, XII, 426.

2. MSA has approximately 2,500 members; 50 percent are professors, 20 percent graduate students, and 15 percent each are employed by industry and by governmental agencies. There are around 1,350 subscribers. Both groups receive the bimonthly *American Mineralogist*, and the latter receive *Reviews in Mineralogy*, which consists of one or two major paper-bound volumes (400-700 pages)

per year on topics in mineralogy, crystallography, petrology, and/or geochemistry.

3. Paul H. Ribbe. "Mammon and Prestige in Earth Science Departments." *American Mineralogist* 73 (1988): 1221-34.

4. Paul H. Ribbe. "Assessment of Prestige and Price of Professional Publications." *American Mineralogist* 73 (1988): 449-69.

5. Paul H. Ribbe. "Assessment of Prestige and Price of Professional Publications: Corrections and Additions." *American Mineralogist* 74 (1989): in press.

6. Eugene Garfield. "English Spoken Here." *The Scientist*, 7 September 1987, 9.

7. See Note 4, above, p. 450 for details of other selection criteria.

8. *Journal Citation Reports* 19 (1985): 7A.

9. Eugene Garfield. "Citation Analysis as a Tool in Journal Evaluation." *Science* 178 (1972): 471-9.

10. *Journal Citation Reports* 20 (1986): 10B.

11. *Journal Citation Reports* 19 (1985): 12A.

12. Eugene Garfield. "Earth Science Journals: What They Cite and What Cites Them," in his *Essays of an Information Scientist*, vol. 5 (Philadelphia: ISI Press, 1981-82), 791-800.

13. L. V. Jones, G. Lindzey, and P. E. Coggeshall, eds. *Mathematical and Physical Sciences. V. Geoscience Programs*, in their *An Assessment of Research-Doctorate Programs in the United States* (Washington: National Academy Press, 1982).

14. Figures 3a and 3b from Figures 12b and 9 in Note 3, above, p. 1229 and p. 1226, respectively.

15. See Note 4, above, Fig. 4, p. 457.

16. Note 4, above, Fig. 3c on p. 457; cf. Table 2.

17. This subject is discussed in detail—see Note 3, above, p. 1229-31.

18. For the sociology of this phenomenon, see D. Crane. *Invisible Colleges: Diffusion of Knowledge in Scientific Communities* (Chicago: University of Chicago Press, 1972).

19. Data from Table 3, p. 458, Note 4, above.

20. K. Bowker. Letter to the Editor. *Science* 238 (1987): 597.

21. Note 4, above, p. 461.

22. C. Holden. "Libraries Stunned by Journal Price Increases." *Science* 237 (1987): 908.

23. See also H. H. Barscall and J. R. Arrington. "Cost of Physics Journals: A Survey." *Bulletin of the American Physical Society* 33 (1988): 1437-47.

SUMMARY SESSION

Kit Kennedy. I recall that at last year's summary session Becky Lenzini, a film buff, aptly placed the issues raised at NASIG within the context of movies. This year I edge away from the world of celluloid and propose a "new" technology for analogy: the technology of print.

So, with apologies to Luigi Pirandello, I offer "Six Ideas in Search of a T-shirt." Imagine, if you will, the lowly and unadorned T-shirt.

> T-shirt number one: UPGRADE THE USER
> Number two: THE GREATEST CONTRIBUTION TO SCHOLARSHIP SINCE COFFEE . . . (flip side: CD-ROM)
> Number three: YOU SAY PROFIT, I SAY SURPLUS
> T-shirt number four: YOU SAY SURPLUS, I SAY PROFIT (flip side: MAMMON AND PRESTIGE)
> Number five: ONE MORE VEHICLE FOR INFORMATION
> The Final T-shirt: MY KINGDOM FOR A PALM TREE[1]

While messages on T-shirts can be witty, immediate, outrageous, confusing, exclusionary, amusing, political, or sometimes offensive, ultimately the impact of the message recedes or fades. By contrast, I believe, what will not fade are the issues raised here at NASIG. And the issues will not fade because they are important, complex, economic, ethical, pervasive, and tough, very tough.

---

1. The symbol of a palm tree on a registration badge designated a member of the local arrangements committee.

We articulate ideas within the context of our own experience and perspective. It is in this drawing upon experience and perspective that Vicky Reich and John Tagler have generously agreed to participate. They will select a few of the issues discussed during the past several days and share their reflections.

First, let me introduce Vicky Reich. Vicky is currently Head of the Serials Department at Stanford University, a position she has held for two years. Her prior experience includes professional positions at the National Agriculture Library and the Library of Congress. Vicky is active in several ALA committees as well as the Society for Scholarly Publishing (SSP). Vicky offers her remarks in the context of scholarly publishing.

Vicky Reich. Thank you, Kit. I am here to present a summary of the conference. The quickest summary I can give you is that I have made a lot of new friends and that I have had a good time. Since Tina indicated that having a good time was the most important thing we were to do, I have done my bit.

This meeting brought together scholars, librarians, vendors, and publishers. Although, throughout the course of modern scholarship, these four communities have been working in parallel toward the very broad common goal of trying to help us understand our universe, we have only met during these past four decades when we absolutely *had* to, to get business done. That is changing. Within the past two or three years there have been an increasing number of activities which have had as their explicit goal to bring all four communities towards a common view of the economics of scholarship. This conference has been one of those activities. I am going to summarize this meeting by outlining what I see as the challenges for each of these four communities—the scholars, the librarians, the publishers, and the vendors—and then I am briefly going to summarize the activities.

The first thing I am going to do is disagree with Gillian Page's statement that the problem is that librarians need more money. Instead, I think that the basic challenge is that more scholars are alive today than have ever lived; that these scholars, to varying degrees, use and produce information; and that we have an academic system in which the interaction of incentives and opportunities virtually assures that the volume of literature will continue to grow. Both Dr. Menzel and Dr. Schuster alluded to these points. Because of this volume of literature, I see at least three challenges for scholars: fraud, access, and cost.

Dr. Schuster mentioned fraud. An increasing number of fraud cases have been reported in science and medicine over the past couple of years, and one might think of fraud as a bad response to the academic incentive and reward system.

Access to literature is the second challenge, and for scientists the challenge is *fast* access. (To give a personal example, the recent Utah cold fusion experiment was widely distributed by FAX and E-mail a good two months before it ever showed up in print. It was even available to people such as myself who do not do cold fusion research.) Dr. Menzel mentioned the half-life of literature. Dr. Popkin talked about the humanities literature, and what I got from his talk was that without moral resources they would not even be able to find most of their research in order to publish it! I think he was being a little bit facetious.

Costs are the third challenge. I think that Dr. Ribbe is an exception in that most scholars are not aware of the cost of their literature because we have a system whereby the financial responsibility for the acquisition of these materials is separate from those who benefit by the materials that librarians obtain. There are some historical examples of disciplines that have been aware of their literature: geologists for one; physicists for another; and mathematicians. The challenge for librarians is that we are very much aware of how much information costs, and that is very scary. The scary part is that we are unable to maintain the historical levels of collection development, which is how prestige is measured. If you want to be an ARL library you have to have so many volumes, and volume count is also how we measure our value to our universities. So the fear is, how will these changing levels of collection development affect our services and programs? David Cohen mentioned that we really know very little about how libraries are used.

The challenge to the publishers is to stay in business. The small publishers are challenged to retain any share of a market that is increasingly going to the larger publishers. Alain Hénon challenged smaller publishers to use technologies more effectively, although larger publishers realize that the current market is really as large as it is going to get. They need to find new markets and new products to sell in order to continue to make money.

I see, too, that the same challenge exists for vendors. Their challenge is to stay in business. In the workshops "Waiting for Nodough" with Dan Tonkery and John Merriman and "The Thor Inventory Ruling: Fact or Fiction?" with Don Jaeger, Lenore Wilkas and Marcia Anderson, the dilemma for the vendors was clear. They are caught between publishers who are trying to make money (or a surplus) and librarians who are stretching every dollar.

Now I will talk about what actions are being taken. For scholars, as I said, the challenges are fraud, access, and cost. As was just mentioned, some scientific organizations such as NIH are recommending that people stand for tenure only on the basis of their *best* work. This approach is actually in response to fraud and not in response to the price of literature; but you can see very easily that the two are connected, and if one is solved, the impact on the other will be great. Many universities are writing ethical guidelines. Stanford has them, and the American Medical Association just a few weeks ago had a meeting in Chicago to discuss fraud in scientific research.

The second challenge was access. Scientists are using FAX and E-mail. I also want to share with you that scientists are starting electronic journals, but that it is mostly for speed of access, not because they are concerned about costs. Two recent examples are *Computer Science in Economics and Management*, edited by someone in Amsterdam, and a second journal on computer-human interactions that is coming out of Scotland. You can see, again, that this will probably have some economic impact on the cost of scholarly literature, but that it is in response to a different, although related, problem.

Then we have cost and we have Dr. Ribbe who is looking at cost along with Henry Barschall, a physicist.

What are librarians doing to address these challenges? We are doing mostly what we do best: we are having meetings. Deana Astle very well summarized the activities of NASIG, SSP, RTSD and MLA. We have the action agendas from ARL. We have Marcia

Tuttle's newsletter; the newsletter of the RTSD P/VLR Task Force on Serials Pricing; and Katina Strauch's newsletter, *Against the Grain*. Alain Hénon mentioned an article in the *Chronicle of Higher Education* by Dick Dougherty calling for university libraries to cooperate with university presses in starting alternative publications. Publishers think this is an incredibly naive idea. Mary Weed (Springer-Verlag) alluded to how much capital it takes to start up a scholarly journal. Nonetheless, this is beginning to happen. A very good example, a very exciting example, is coming out of the Johns Hopkins University Medical Library and the Johns Hopkins University Press, a project that they are calling "Knowledge Management."

Yesterday we heard about CD-ROMs and we heard that they are expensive but effective. I was thinking that, if you take into consideration the cost of users' time and how much more satisfied they seem to be with that technology, CD-ROMs might be cheaper than mainframe databases or the print indices.

Also in response to our challenges, we heard Jan Anderson and October Ivins discuss whether it is real or false economy to consolidate serial acquisitions with a single vendor. I think we could probably have a week's discussion on that alone.

What are publishers doing? I do not know what the smaller publishers are doing. (That is one of the things I am still trying to learn about.) I know that the larger publishers have decreased the number of new titles that they might ordinarily start. They also say they have held down costs for the current year in direct response to market pressure.

What are vendors doing? They are competing for business with teeth and claws and are buying each other out. They are trying to help librarians and publishers, both, understand their role in this very complex process. Very selfishly, I hope that all the vendors succeed and stay in business. I wish them the best of luck.

For the future, I am hopeful that our four communities will evolve a new, more effective model of scholarly communication. As a serials librarian, I find this a little bit like being on a white water rafting trip about to fall overboard at any moment. I keep in mind what you are supposed to do when you fall overboard: you are supposed to point your feet downstream, push off from the rocks, and remember to look out and enjoy the scenery. That is what I have been trying to do. Thank you.

Kit Kennedy. John Tagler is Director of Marketing at Elsevier Science Publishers. He has been with Elsevier for twelve years. John has an MLS from Pratt and worked first as a librarian at the National Foundation of the March of Dimes and then at IEEE for four years. John is a member of the NASIG Continuing Education Committee and is active in the Society for Scholarly Publishing and various library and publishing organizations.

John Tagler. Since I was compiling my notes for this presentation last night while everybody was "discoeing," I hope my efforts have been well placed. When Kit invited me she said "a short presentation." As I started compiling my notes, they got longer and longer, so perhaps rather than the paddle, we really needed a hook here.

As I have sat through the sessions these past two days, I began to think of the progress that has been made over the last couple of meetings. This is my third meeting. I regret that I am not among that elite number who have attended all four, but I have really seen changes over the last three years, and I think it is a real progress.

Two years ago we had a great deal of division between the publishers and the librarians. There were a lot of accusations, a lot of misunderstandings, and at the close of the meeting they were really divided camps. There was a real effort last year to mend some of that tension, and I think real progress has been made. We seemed at the end of the session to come to the conclusion that we are part of a much larger scene. The effort this year has been to bring in some of the other players in the game, so to speak. We have invited academics, editors, scientists, and humanities people to give their perspectives. And we have found that there really are no quick, easy solutions. The solution is certainly not going to be in technology. There are a lot of other groups with vested interests—not just publishers; certainly the academic and university administrations are entrenched in many ways—and I think that, even if there is a recognized need for change, it is not going to be rapid.

So where does that leave us? Well, I think it leaves NASIG in a unique position. Mary Helms, Medical Library Association liaison to NASIG, reported yesterday that MLA is now talking about journal prices. Since NASIG was talking about that issue two years ago, I think the membership is in a very good position because of the singleness of purpose and interest in this group. It is a small group and yet represents a very important cross-section. I think it is a very good place to begin to find some solutions.

As publishers we are very eager for some channels, some forums in which we can begin to address some of the things that we are trying to work towards. Certainly the indicators we get from the market show that things have to change. What we have not really been able to discern is in what way. Dr. Menzel was talking about changes in the editorial process. He sees electronic publishing as being a very, very important factor, and we all recognize it, but he also emphasized that some standards are needed. I think that is an area that we have to begin working in. He also pointed out that not only do we need electronic impact at the print or the delivery stage but we also need it at the entry stage, the point of manuscript submission, and we need it at the refereeing stage as well. Now, as I said a little while ago, the indicators are not clear. As publishers we have done research, and if we want to bring these products and services to the market, there is a great deal more investment to be made. Hence we are very much interested in any group or any forum that can help guide us.

We got some indicators from the session on CD-ROM. The product that was discussed yesterday is a bit different from what we deal in: we do have some databases and secondary indexing services that are on CD, but our main concern, of course, is full text, and most of what was addressed in the CD-ROM session was indexes and databases. But there are a couple of very important points that we can learn from.

Joe Michalak mentioned a very basic thing, basic to commercial publishers, namely that we are commercial organizations and will respond. You tell us what you want (or do not want) and how you want it, and we have to respond to that, and if we do not—we as Elsevier, or we as commercial publishers—then someone else will step in to fill that gap. Another point in that regard was Beth Juhl's experience in feedback from the users. After a tentative start, people were enthusiastic about using this new technology and went about it swimmingly. When it came to paying, however, there was a great big question mark. Nobody really seemed to know how much it was worth, who was going to pay, and how they were going to go about paying. So as publishers we have come up against these very same stumbling blocks, and until we get more answers I think we do not really know quite where the technology is going to take us.

In the research that we have done (and we have done research both with scientists as well as with librarians, to try to see what is wanted), we have found that scientists really do not want to be information managers. I think they very much see the librarian as having an even more important role in this. As the channels become more diffuse, as the amount of information continues to grow, as the hierarchy or level or prestige (or whatever you want to call it) of these publications begins to change and expand, I think the role of the librarian as the information manager, as the conduit, will become increasingly important. Similarly, our research indicates that from the publisher's perspective that conduit role will continue to grow. The one overwhelming response we get from the scientists is that peer review and quality control are imperative. As there is more information, there is more and more emphasis on quality. Presuming, therefore, that the publisher adds value for money and is a clearinghouse and a controlling factor in this regard, I think that the publisher's role will continue to grow as well.

Of course, one thing which Gillian Page pointed out and which is very important to keep in mind, is that whereas publishers look at the new technology as a source of new revenues, librarians look at it as a source of cost savings. In fact, it may be neither. I think that technology will be a new dimension and that it may involve the shifting of funds, but it is not the panacea, certainly not in the short term. In the short term we are still looking at price increases and concerns over pricing. Gillian did list ten pricing considerations. If I were compiling the list I probably would have come up with about the same ten. I think the thing to bear in mind is that there is no one model. When you factor her ten points there are enormous variations within any one of those. Price is not a *determining* factor. Page charges are a factor. Advertising is a big factor. At Elsevier we produce some journals for three cents a page. We have other journals that are in the twenty-five cent per page range, and we have journals that are in the forty cent range. We probably have some that are over fifty. But there is variation, and even within a company such as Elsevier there is no single formula, there is no "correct" or "incorrect" pricing. For some libraries, a five thousand dollar journal is very cost-effective; in other libraries, if you gave it to them, they would not want it and could not use it. So cost alone is not really an indicator. Dr. Ribbe certainly gave us some other considerations that should be factored in.

One item that needs to be considered is the ARL survey. I am a bit concerned: I wish some of the methodology had been explained more fully. I would like to have seen some analysis of how the Economic Consulting Service survey was conducted. The survey has been quoted extensively already (this is the season for library meetings). In fact, at a panel that I was on at MLA a couple of weeks ago, a librarian quoted an extremely provocative section of the ARL summary which subsequently was excised from the report. The report has to be used very carefully, and until we have really seen the data, I think it is a bit of a kangaroo court. It is a case of "getting" four sci/tech publishers and making sweeping generalizations without really looking at the data. A number of people have expressed to me that they have doubts about the methodology used by ECS. I also wish they had factored in a number of other publishers—large sci/tech, small sci/tech, the society publishers and some university presses. So the study did seem to me a bit limited in its perspective.

To summarize: My main theme, what I am taking out of this meeting, is that we need to work. We need some solutions. We need at least initial steps in the short term, and basically the only way that we are going to accomplish this is through trust, understanding, more awareness, and more information that we share among ourselves. Thank you.

Kit Kennedy. Well, I lied. There are in fact seven T-shirts, and this is the final one. It says 0-345-34660-2. That happens to be the ISBN for Peter Taylor's marvelous novel *A Summons to Memphis*, and I will do a rough quote from that: "In adversity it is best to live off of your sense of humor."

WORKSHOP SESSION REPORTS

The Commercial Binding Agreement: Partners in Preservation

Martin Gordon
Bruce Jacobsen
Workshop Leaders

Tim McAdam
Recorder

Bruce Jacobsen, Vice President for Bridgeport National Bindery, and Martin Gordon, Serials Librarian at Franklin & Marshall College, presented this workshop on binding and preservation.

Jacobsen and Gordon discussed the Commercial Binding Agreement (CBA). The CBA has a purpose for both the library and the bindery. The CBA provides the library with a consistent, excellent quality of materials preservation within a stable price structure. The CBA also provides the binder with a predictable volume of business to be fulfilled with a clear understanding of expectations and requirements. The CBA should include three elements: technical/administrative needs; materials specification; and binding methodol-

---

Tim McAdam is Head of Acquisitions and Serials, Boston College, O'Neill Library, Chestnut Hill, MA 02167.

© 1990 by The Haworth Press, Inc. All rights reserved.

ogy. The first part, technical/administrative needs, should include components such as pricing structure, loss of materials by binder, pick-up and delivery schedules, invoicing requirements, termination and revision of the CBA, and library acceptance of the finished product. The second part of the CBA should address the quality of materials used, such as thread, paper, adhesive, back lining, boards, coverings, inlays, and foil. All materials used should meet or exceed Library Binding Institute standards.

The third part, methodology, should address the different types of binding available — custom, standard, and economy — and specify the general treatment that materials will receive.

For libraries that have not drafted their own Commercial Binding Agreement, some binderies can provide a Technical Proposal that will address the areas normally included in a CBA. Libraries that wish to draft their own CBA can turn to a variety of resources for assistance: existing CBAs at other institutions; knowledgeable librarians and binders; Library Binding Institute standards; workshops; articles; and common sense. A bibliography citing readings on the binding process was distributed.

A Commercial Binding Agreement should be flexible in order to accommodate the development of improved methods and materials in the binding industry. Both the library and the binder should agree on introducing new methods and materials after testing to ensure quality. It was noted that if a CBA is silent regarding a particular topic, parties to the agreement can rely on LBI standards for that area.

Following the discussion was a slide presentation of the various types of binding options, including side sewing, sew-through-the-fold, double fan adhesive, and other methods. The workshop concluded with a discussion of the advantages and disadvantages of the various methods.

Latest Entry Cataloging As an Option

Bradley Carrington
Mary M. Case

Workshop Leaders

Sharon Scott

Recorder

This workshop, led by Mary M. Case, Head of the Serials Department and Bradley Carrington, Head of the Serials Cataloging Section, both at Northwestern University, focused on Northwestern's use of latest entry cataloging as an alternative to successive entry records in their on-line catalog.

Mary Case began the workshop with an introduction to the history of latest entry cataloging in the United States. Title change practice was first discussed as far back as 1876 when Cutter advocated the use of earliest entry cataloging, or as an option, successive entry. Latest entry cataloging was presented as an alternative sometime around 1908 and officially sanctioned by the 1949 edition of the *A.L.A. Cataloging Rules*. The 1967 *Anglo-American Cataloging Rules*, however, called for successive entry catalog records. Since the Library of Congress did not adopt this rule until 1971, the history of successive entry cataloging is relatively short.

In a card catalog environment, latest entry cataloging is cumbersome to maintain because of the need for constant revision and refiling of card sets. Successive entry catalog records, although easier to maintain in a card catalog, have caused a proliferation of records.

Sharon Scott is Senior Serials Cataloger, University of Arizona, Tucson, AZ 85721.

Indeed, one can view the number of rule interpretations and modifications of the rules dealing with title changes as an attempt to cope with record proliferation. Automation has also led to a reevaluation of the rules, since automation makes it easy to provide as many access points as needed.

In the early 1970s, Northwestern converted all of its serials to NOTIS. Since Northwestern catalogers had begun using successive entry cataloging in 1971, both latest entry and successive entry cataloging were present in the NOTIS database. They made no attempt to convert old latest entry catalog records to successive entry. In 1985, because of the great number of successive entry records being created and the number of what appeared to be meaningless title changes generating these records, Northwestern staff began to evaluate their use of successive entry cataloging. They adapted latest entry cataloging practice in the spring of 1985 and have created approximately 600 latest entry records in the last four years.

The next section of the workshop, presented by Brad Carrington, was a discussion of the actual rules for latest entry cataloging as developed by Northwestern. These rules are intended to supplement AACR2; some rules are additions to the existing cataloging code, while others are replacements. The Latest Entry Cataloging Rules (LEC) do not change the determination as to whether a title has changed; existing AACR2 rules still apply.

Criteria for determining the application of LEC rules include the following: the numbering must continue (if numbering starts over, a new record is created); the title must be classified; splits and mergers are not candidates for latest entry cataloging; and the title history must not be too complicated (this decision is left to the individual cataloger).

Before looking at the rules individually, Carrington stressed that all information in the body of the description (except for enumeration/chronology) is based on the latest issue. This rule supports the philosophy of having the latest information available to better serve a variety of users, including acquisitions staff. The presentation of rules and sample cataloging problem worked out by the group stimulated an interesting dialogue among all present. Questions and comments on the effects of latest entry cataloging were wide-ranging.

The final portion of this workshop was a report on a user survey conducted at Northwestern to determine the patron's ability to interpret cataloging records. A questionnaire was developed in cooperation with reference staff. The questionnaire asked the user for specific information about five different serial titles in Northwestern's catalog: two cataloged by successive entry rules; two cataloged by latest entry rules; and one which had no title change. User response demonstrated overwhelmingly that patrons understand latest entry better than successive entry records. Detailed holdings information is much easier to ascertain when held together by latest entry records. The presenters stressed, however, that it was difficult to devise unambiguous questions and that the survey is considered exploratory at this time.

Where Are Serials in Your Organization Chart?

Terry Ann Sayler
Carol Schaafsma

Workshop Leaders

Miriam Palm

Recorder

Terry Ann Saylor, Head of the Serials Unit, Acquisitions Department, at University of Maryland at College Park, began the workshop with a *Jeopardy*-like game.

Answer: The Golden Age in France, the seventeenth century. *Question*: When was the first serial published? (*Des Savants* began in 1640, is still being published, and has had only one title change.)

Answer: The Centennial of the American Revolution in 1876. *Question*: When was ALA founded?

Answer: The Great Depression of the 1930s. *Question*: When did the Periodicals Section of ALA write the first serials manual and mandate separate departments to manage this format?

Answer: The Cold War of the 1950s. *Question*: When was the first newsletter for serials librarians published? (*Serials Slants* was published in 1956.)

Answer: Sixty to forty. *Question*: What proportion of libraries included in a 1984 ARL survey have serials departments and what proportion do not?

Saylor elaborated that "technical services" as a specialized area of library practice was not formed until the 1930s; before that time,

---

Miriam Palm is Assistant Chief, Serials Department, Stanford University Libraries, Stanford, CA 94305.

© 1990 by The Haworth Press, Inc. All rights reserved.

libraries typically consisted of acquisitions, catalog, reference, and circulation departments. Until recently, organization by "form," which centralizes work where records and expertise are housed, has been viewed as achieving the goal of better service. Over the past ten years, however, libraries have come to view organization by "function" as more economical, especially in view of the expanded access made possible by automation. Sayler commented that new administrators often wish to make a distinctive mark on their organizations and frequently select serials to be centralized or decentralized for "political" reasons.

Carol Schaafsma, Head of the Serials Department at the University of Hawaii, listed several factors that can be used to justify arrangement by either format or function. For example, large organizations may wish to concentrate staff expertise. Automation allows concurrent access to the same record at multiple locations. "We've always done it that way" provides a precedent, but the reasons should be reevaluated. Other factors can include physical arrangement (is the collection in a single building or dispersed among branches?); the history and abilities of the current staff; and whether staff presently are being used in the most beneficial manner.

With this background, Sayler described the disbanding of the Serials Department at the University of Maryland in April of 1981. Staff were moved into other existing departments and formed smaller serials processing units within Acquisitions, Original Cataloging, Bibliographic Support, Catalog Management, and the Retrospective Conversion Project. Sayler attributed the successful outcome of this dispersal to the informal communications network that continued among the serials processing staff. Projects that also helped keep this network in place included the in-house serials list, automated cataloging on OCLC, and the implementation of automated check-in on GEAC.

Sayler, who joined the library after the change took place, offered the following assessment of the current arrangement. She reported a lack of leadership and formal coordination of serials activities, in part because the change was implemented with little consultation with the affected staff, and also because the new supervisors of these staff had little experience with serials. Staff in public services units often do not know whom to consult when they encounter problems or have questions. On the positive side, materials do move and work is accomplished. The previous view of serials staff as specialists unwilling to interact with other units has disappeared because people in many departments now benefit more directly from their expertise. For example, a broader knowledge of serials payments has helped both daily processing and the annual audit to proceed smoothly.

Schaafsma described how the University of Hawaii Libraries formed a central Serials Department in August 1977. The grouping of serials functions into a single department was precipitated by a physical rearrangement which made it more logical to unite serials receipts and payments functions. As automation increased, the receipts staff used OCLC to resolve problems and progressed to performing some types of copy cataloging. Their success in eliminating a cataloging backlog of 5,000 titles led the monographs receipts unit to adopt a similar "cataloging in receipt" procedure. The Periodicals Room, binding preparation, and Microform Room gradually also became part of the Serials Department, giving the staff a successful and gratifying range of processing and public service duties.

Coordination of cataloging policies requires vigilance in a distributed environment. In addition, some processing, primarily of non-Roman languages, has remained separated because generalists cannot be expected to deal with such specialized processing needs. Training of new staff involves a large initial investment, since it is long and complex. Schaafsma attributed the success of the department to the experienced, long-term staff and the new challenges that the team approach has offered them. She also applauded their receptiveness to change, and noted that they continue to adjust the organization to respond to needs and good ideas. She expects that, in the future, there will be further standardization and emphasis on consistency, and that receipts will be dispersed to the branch libraries and special collections.

Discussion after the presentations centered on how, in function-based or decentralized environments, serials expertise is transmitted to staff performing the work, if they report to supervisors who are not serials experts.

Non-Print Serials and Title Waves

Marilyn Geller
Anna Wang

Workshop Leaders

Marlene Sue Heroux

Recorder

Two presentations of interest to serials catalogers were offered as one workshop during the NASIG conference. Anna Wang (Ohio State University) delivered a paper on the special problems of acquiring and cataloging non-print serials. Marilyn Geller (MIT) presented a study of serial title changes.

NON-PRINT SERIALS

Wang defined non-print serials to include remote access computer files, CD-ROM databases, microforms, and multi-media publications. CD-ROM acquisitions and bibliographic tools are particularly welcome additions to the profession because of the powerful capabilities of Boolean searching; the ability to download customized files for bibliographies, orders, and catalogs; and the lack of high telecommunications charges. Products utilizing Hypertext have features such as the capability to highlight titles owned by the library and to restrict searching to these items alone.

Wang's presentation focused on the issues of cost, licensing agreements, check-in records, software installation, cataloging, preservation, and storage. With regard to cost, some publishers offer discounts to subscribers of both print and CD-ROM versions of

Marlene Sue Heroux is an Account Services Representative for EBSCO Subscription Services. Her address is 1148 Briarcliff Road #2, Atlanta, GA 30306.

© 1990 by The Haworth Press, Inc. All rights reserved.

a title. Differential pricing is also a factor in the mounting of databases for use in local area networks (LAN). Both cost and licensing agreements influence decisions about making back-up copies of software: Wang suggested that librarians get written permission to download software into local systems. Licensing agreements can be handled either up front as part of the ordering process or after the fact as part of receiving.

Check-in records for non-print serials should contain details such as the medium, size, number of disks expected, accompanying templates or documentation, and the return policy for leased materials. It is also a good idea to include the policy for defective or lost disks.

Cataloging decisions include whether to catalog, which may depend in part on ownership status of the material, and what level of cataloging to choose. ALA guidelines recommend that microcomputer software have the same level of subject access as other material. Analytical cataloging may be useful. Since the MARC format for machine-readable data files (MRDF) does not contain 780/785 fields, Wang suggested using the 730 field for linking notes.

A library may wish to make pamphlet binders for floppy disks and CD's, depending on the sturdiness of publisher-supplied containers. Passage through security systems will not erase data; however, circulation desensitizers may damage software.

Looking toward the future, format integration will address cataloging format weaknesses. In addition, a NISO committee is developing standards for CD-ROM bibliographic citations. As more libraries acquire the hardware to use CD-ROM products, and as LAN technology improves, resources sharing for multi-institutional and consortium use will be a key issue.

TITLE WAVES

Because there is little in library literature that addresses *why* serials change their titles, Geller's initiative is an interesting addition to serials research. Her study concentrated primarily on title changes among scholarly publications in an attempt to discern explanatory patterns. Title change categories include: merger of two or more marginally successful publications; splitting of a single title as a discipline matures; changes in scope, publisher, editor, language, and/or frequency; "goofs"; and "mysterious" changes. The latter category contains all changes that do not fit elsewhere.

Both publishers and libraries may benefit from title changes. On the publisher's side, changing a serials' title allows greater responsiveness to the market. In rare cases, a merger might lead to increased revenues, if two less popular publications had been suffering losses. From the library perspective, a merger means one less title to buy, process, and preserve. Furthermore, if the change more accurately reflects the journal's content, access can be enhanced, especially in online public access catalogs with keyword searching. It was also pointed out that title changes provide job security for librarians!

There are drawbacks to changing a journal's title even from the publisher's perspective. A title change (done well) requires publishers to notify subscribers, agents, and abstracting and indexing services. They must apply for a new ISSN. Design of a new cover and logo can be expensive. Changes are also costly for libraries. Titles that split can require additional funding to purchase two publications in an era of increasingly tight budgets. It is expensive to change acquisitions, cataloging and binding files. Shelving can be problematic when journals are arranged alphabetically by title.

Geller emphasized the importance of alerting publishers to the negative impact of title changes on libraries. When changes are warranted, she stressed that publishers be provided with guidelines regarding numbering, lettering, and other issues so as to minimize impact. She recommended further research into the topic, including impact studies of title changes on users. During discussion, a participant suggested that future research might separate commercial from scholarly publication.

Serials Analysis for Budget and Collection Review As Well As Cooperative Development

Christie Degener
Audrey J. Kidder
Cheryl Riley

Workshop Leaders

Dana D'Andraia

Recorder

In this workshop, three librarians reported on serials collection analyses undertaken at three separate academic libraries.

Audrey J. Kidder, Fordham Health Sciences Librarian at Wright State University, began her presentation with a few comments about the Dayton Acquistions Cooperative, founded in 1976 by nine Dayton area health sciences libraries. The cooperative was established so that each member library could develop its own unique collection while also having ready access to in-depth city-wide resources. Members enjoy free interlending with a three to four day average delivery rate, plus a FAX rush service. A full description of the cooperative was published in the January 1977 *Bulletin of the Medical Library Association*.

Studies conducted in 1984 and 1989 assessed member libraries' holdings by subject and number of titles. The 1989 study also evaluated the effect of a 1984 revision in subject headings and attempted to determine whether budget constraints were having an

Dana D'Andraia is Head of Acquisitions, University of California Library, Box 19557, University of California at Irvine, Irvine, CA 92713.

© 1990 by The Haworth Press, Inc. All rights reserved.

effect on members' ability to cooperate. Both studies revealed the success of the cooperative. Although serials costs have increased by 90 percent since 1984, collectively no titles were lost, although some libraries did lose non-unique titles.

One of the many benefits experienced by the member libraries is the validation of their collections. Library administrators have signed contracts making an institutional commitment to collect in specified subject areas and to cancel unique titles only with the agreement of all members. Libraries also refrain from cancelling a duplicate title until a member library has committed to collecting it.

Cheryl Riley, Catalog Maintenance Head at Central Missouri State University Library, described a budget history database which she devised for the purpose of serial cost projection. She created the file from a Faxon SCOPE report by using SMARTS software, which integrates spreadsheet and word processing functions. It is easy to add fields to a SMARTS file, all fields are sortable, and a library can run complex searches on a large number of records. One of Riley's handouts was a spreadsheet color-coded to show seven decision points devised to handle suspended, ceased, or gift titles in the SMARTS format.

The database included payment information for approximately 3,000 titles to which Central Missouri has subscribed since 1979. CSMU subject specialists, who for the first time had information on current prices, payment history, and percentage increases, were able to use the report for journal retention decisions.

With the help of two College of Business faculty members, Riley transferred data from the file to the campus mainframe and developed a statistical model to project future journal costs. One benefit of the analysis is the ability to justify budget needs for the university administration; to date, the library has not had to engage in deselection because of budget deficits.

Christie Degener, Serials Librarian at the Health Sciences Library of the University of North Carolina at Chapel Hill, described a project conducted with two other Health Sciences librarians. Using their PERLINE automated serials system, they devised an evaluation methodology based on thirteen weighted categories, including indexing; subject; relation to collection; user request; cost; language; issuing association; regional availability; publisher, borrowing history; geographic scope; refereeing policy; and citation data. After coding, the criteria were recorded online as a string of data in one field.

The library conducted a cancellation review by dividing the collection into eighteen subsets and producing lists based on the codes. Lists of potential candidates for cancellation were distributed to faculty and staff for comment. After final cancellation decisions were made, library personnel updated the records and distributed lists of cancelled titles.

The same method is used to evaluate potential new journals for the collection. Titles being considered for purchase are input into the data base, coded with the same values, and compared to titles already in the collection.

Questions during the discussion period covered systems, software, weighing methods, and responses to the studies by librarians, faculty, and publishers. Each presenter plans to publish her work in the library literature.

Creative Strategies for Serials Management: Current Awareness Services

Mary E. Ito
Susan K. Kinnell
Pat Napier
Jeffrey Serena
Workshop Leaders

Rebecca Schwartzkopf
Recorder

Pat Napier, Current Awareness Librarian at Napier Polytechnic, Edinburgh, Scotland, began this session by describing her experience with two types of current awareness publications for serials at her institution. *Current Awareness Bulletin for Education* is provided primarily for faculty members at Napier Polytechnic. Produced through a database management program, this bulletin is arranged by subject and includes bibliographic information, keyword descriptors, and location information for each article.

The second type of services is a compilation of tables of contents from journals. This format is appropriate when only a few clients require current awareness service on a particular subject. For this reason, Napier Polytechnic uses the copied contents method for its management and tourism departments.

According to Napier, the key to successful current awareness publications is familiarity with the intended market. Questions concerning other products currently available, audience, and production costs should be carefully addressed during the planning stages.

Rebecca Schwartzkopf is Periodical/Map Librarian, Mankato State University, Mankato, MN 56002.

© 1990 by The Haworth Press, Inc. All rights reserved.

Questions from the workshop participants concerned the day-to-day process of collecting information for the publications. Napier explained that a cooperative relationship with the serials check-in department is the key to timely identification of materials.

Mary Ito, Serials Librarian at California Institute of Technology, presented the second session, entitled "Beyond Serials Control." Ito described the development and operation of Caltech's online current awareness system, TOC/DOC (Table of Contents/ Document Delivery). The system provides online access to indexing for approximately 1,800 scientific and technical journals available at Caltech and has filled over 65,000 article requests. Students and faculty access this current awareness system through the campus local area network. Users make their request via an online form, and Caltech's document delivery system provides the articles within forty-eight hours.

Caltech receives weekly SCISEARCH tapes from the Institute for Scientific Information and uses these records to index its journal collection. When the tapes arrive, citations for Caltech journals are stripped from the tape and incorporated into the TOC/DOC database. In addition, Caltech staff integrate publisher changes and local data into the system.

The TOC/DOC database uses BRS command language to search by journal title, author title, and date. A separate database is maintained for each year beginning in 1987.

Ito outlined problems with the present system: (1) title data entered from the SCISEARCH tapes are not always consistent with AACR2 cataloging rules; (2) typographical errors in the ISI tapes enter the TOC/DOC system; and (3) hardware capabilities limit the amount of information that can be stored in the database. Planned enhancements include an increased title base, improved retrieval capability, and SDI searching.

Jeffrey Serena, Managing Editor at ABC-CLIO, and Susan Kinnell, Online Coordinator and Development Editor at ABC-CLIO, ended the workshop by discussing future implications of resource sharing programs. Serena began by outlining the key elements of a resource sharing program and the impact of these elements on libraries and publishers. The five elements are:

1. determining the subscription base for participants;
2. cataloging all journals to provide access;
3. identifying articles through indexes and abstracts;
4. establishing a lending balance among participants; and
5. establishing the means to facilitate rapid lending.

According to Serena, resource sharing will serve to escalate rather than reduce journal costs, since prices will continue to rise as fewer libraries subscribe to each title. The increased specialization of journals will also drive prices higher.

Serena views the sharing of resources as an evolutionary process toward centralized library facilities, an inevitable consequence of the information explosion. The question now facing us is: How will libraries and publishers adapt to their new functions?

Kinnell carried Serena's model one step further with her vision of the total electronic library system. She foresees enormous regional electronic storage facilities which will provide resources to traditional information agencies such as libraries, historical societies, and government offices. The technology needed for this type of information transfer is available now: telecommunications, FAX machines, high density TV, and online data transmission will all play an important role in the electronic library of the future. Kinnell believes that the library of the future may change our present description of a journal. The electronic version may be produced article-by-article rather than issue-by-issue.

Kinnell's revelation stirred lively discussion about libraries of the future and the evolving role of librarians and publishers. Participants identified consistency of online systems and standard search terminology as keys to accessing information in the future.

The publisher's role within the scheme of electronic information systems is uncertain: How will publishers be reimbursed when access is online? Electronic transfer of information will also change some traditional concepts — for example, the concept of browsing a journal.

Kinnell closed the session by describing the personal computer of the future, which will write, file, and organize all information needs through voice command.

To Bid or Not to Bid: Is It Still a Choice?

Lawrence R. Keating II
Nancy H. Rogers

Workshop Leaders

Bill Wilmering

Recorder

Nancy Rogers, General Manager of EBSCO Subscription Services, opened the workshop with an introductory statement noting that the issue of bidding for periodical subscription service has been with libraries for some time. It was the modus operandi before World War II but later fell into disfavor. Librarians generally believe that bidding hampers the freedom and efficiency of the acquisitions process. The bidding process is labor-intensive because of the difficulty of writing good bid specifications. It is also troublesome because of the concern about disruption of service and the difficulty of documenting value added by agents who emphasize service and good business practices. Many librarians question if there are any benefits, because the general consensus is that the costs saved by procuring the lowest bidder are lost by costs incurred in the bidding process.

Most often bidding is mandated for state institutions by statewide rules and regulations. One survey shows that as many as 75 percent of public libraries and 63 percent of school libraries bid. Academic libraries, on the other hand, show much lower percentage of bid requirements for subscription purchases. In one survey, only one

Bill Wilmering is Head of Serial Record, National Library of Medicine, Bethesda, MD 20894.

dors and evaluating from performance whether the choice was wise. Bidding can, with careful planning, yield benefits to the library. It can give the best possible service at the most reasonable cost. It works best where there is a history and tradition of contract bidding because that gives a foundation on which subsequent actions may be laid. It also works well when there is a good working relationship between the library and the purchasing department/agent.

To Bid or Not to Bid:
Is It Still a Choice?

Lawrence R. Keating II
Nancy H. Rogers

Workshop Leaders

Bill Wilmering

Recorder

Nancy Rogers, General Manager of EBSCO Subscription Services, opened the workshop with an introductory statement noting that the issue of bidding for periodical subscription service has been with libraries for some time. It was the modus operandi before World War II but later fell into disfavor. Librarians generally believe that bidding hampers the freedom and efficiency of the acquisitions process. The bidding process is labor-intensive because of the difficulty of writing good bid specifications. It is also troublesome because of the concern about disruption of service and the difficulty of documenting value added by agents who emphasize service and good business practices. Many librarians question if there are any benefits, because the general consensus is that the costs saved by procuring the lowest bidder are lost by costs incurred in the bidding process.

Most often bidding is mandated for state institutions by statewide rules and regulations. One survey shows that as many as 75 percent of public libraries and 63 percent of school libraries bid. Academic libraries, on the other hand, show much lower percentage of bid requirements for subscription purchases. In one survey, only one

Bill Wilmering is Head of Serial Record, National Library of Medicine, Bethesda, MD 20894.

institution in a group of 46 academic libraries was required by state law to bid.

Recently there are signs of change toward mandatory bidding regulations, particularly in the Northeast, the Middle Atlantic states, and the Southeast. Reasons for this change include general budget problems in the states and the fact that state purchasing agents are beginning to exercise guidelines and rules which have not always been enforced in the past. In some states, librarians have been unsuccessful in fighting this trend, while in other states librarians have been able to turn the trend around and defeat initiatives to mandate bidding. The most successful tactic has been to document the cost. For example, in one institution, a study showed that it would cost $3.50 per record just to change vendor source information in the serial record. Today there is a general gloom in library circles because successful reversal of the trend to bid is difficult, and many librarians panic when confronted by mandatory bidding.

Being prepared is good therapy for the bidding panic. Librarians should know the regulations and guidelines under which their institution operates. By quietly identifying and studying the rules, they can be forearmed should the ax fall with a directive to bid. Librarians should be prepared either to live with and accept the rules or to combat the decision with cogent arguments based on statistics and documentation. Unfortunately, library literature is very weak on the subject of bidding: the most recent landmark article is dated 1980. As with all disaster preparedness, librarians should contemplate possible actions in preparation for eventualities. Advance planning is especially appropriate when a new encumbant enters a purchasing position, because new officials most often question what has been done in the past. Another precautionary action is to follow existing purchasing procedures to the letter of the law. It is often minor errors which raise questions about the overall procedures.

Nancy Rogers is preparing a survey of bidding requirements in the 50 states and expects to publish the results in volume 4 of *Advances in Library Administration*.

Larry Keating of the M.D. Anderson Library of the University of Houston told of that institution's success in the bid process. Bidding can be a highly effective means of serial procurement because it forces librarians to think about their needs. It can reduce service charges and can encourage vendors to provide services that they might not develop on their own. Bidding can also be disastrous if service is disrupted, if it increases staff cost and work load, or if the contract is made by a purchasing agent without the advice and consent of the library.

Preliminary planning is important in the contracting process. The size of the collection, the dollar amount, the number and type of titles, as well as their place of origin, all influence the bid design. A single award contract has the advantage of consolidation and brings to bear the power of volume buying. A multiple award contract spreads the business among a number of vendors and permits performance comparisons. From the beginning, the purchasing agent and the library need to work together. Too often the results are unacceptable to the library if the purchasing agent makes the award solely on the bottom line and not on the basis of cost and service.

Following the planning stage, the bidding process proceeds to the writing of the proposal. Often a new contract can be modeled on those in place in other institutions, unless the specifications are considered proprietary by the institution with the first award. Contracts vary from generic to extremely specific. In either style there are two important considerations. First, contracts should specify that the awardee be able to document the vendor's ability to provide the service. Second, all contracts should be submitted to legal counsel for review.

After the proposals go out, the library evaluates the responses received. In addition to the mandatory requirements given in the law, the library should have the option to weigh the proposals based on documentation of previous service and performance. During the bid evaluation it is essential that librarian and purchasing agent work harmoniously together.

Transitions need not be traumatic. It is, of course, easier to switch subscriptions in an automated environment with the capability for mass updates. After award and transition, the librarian needs to develop methods of evaluating performance. Evaluation completes the bidding and award cycle by measuring how well the requirements are met.

Bidding, then, can be viewed as simply a more formalized version of the everyday activities of a serials librarian: choosing vendors and evaluating from performance whether the choice was wise. Bidding can, with careful planning, yield benefits to the library. It can give the best possible service at the most reasonable cost. It works best where there is a history and tradition of contract bidding because that gives a foundation on which subsequent actions may be laid. It also works well when there is a good working relationship between the library and the purchasing department/agent.

Waiting for "Nodough": The Future of Service Charges

John Merriman
Dan Tonkery
Workshop Leaders

Margaret M. Merryman
Recorder

The agent's perspective on the effect of vendor competition, increasing service demands by libraries, and changes in the way charges may be computed in the future were the subjects of this workshop.

Dan Tonkery, President and CEO of Readmore, began the workshop by outlining the subscription agent's current philosophy on service charges. Also participating was John Merriman, Director of Blackwell's Periodicals Division.

Tonkery opened by pointing out that agents apply service charges to cover their operating costs; that these charges are based on the publisher's list price; and that charges have declined over the past three years. Competition has had more impact than any other factor on reducing service charges. But while service charges have dropped, libraries are requesting more services, such as interfacing with automated systems, reports, analyses, and MARC records. A key factor is that subscription vendors are losing money on some transactions. For instance, Tonkery described the typical agent transaction as a journal with a list price of $100. The agent charges 3 percent ($3.00); the library pays $103; the agent pays the pub-

Margaret M. Merryman is Chief of Acquisitions, U.S. Geological Survey Libraries, Reston, VA 22092.

lishers $93 and retains $10 to service the subscription; but the cost to service the subscription is $14, resulting in a loss to the agent of $4. Detailed discussion followed on the reasons agents are willing to absorb the loss on some titles.

Tonkery reported that service charge rates depend on the title mix of an account. Science and technology titles and foreign titles, which are generally more expensive, offset the lower prices of humanities and social science titles. Additionally, agent competition is holding down service charge rates to artificial levels. At present, agents are sometimes more concerned with gaining market share than with making profit on an account. To illustrate this, Tonkery said that twenty years ago there were approximately forty agents; ten years ago there were twelve; and the number continues to decline. After the battle for market share is won, the remaining agents will be able to raise service charge rates. Tonkery asserted that there is a growing pressure to increase rates but that no agent wants to be the first.

Next, Tonkery showed a graph illustrating that the agent's revenue per subscription increases as the average price of a journal rises. Since the agent must make approximately $14 on a subscription to break even, any subscription below about $140 is losing money. The agent, then, looks for libraries that have a mix of titles in the higher-priced range (science and technology) that will support the lower-priced titles (humanities and social sciences).

Tonkery gave a vendor's perspective on claiming, which is one of the service demands that is rising rapidly. Increasing numbers of libraries are using automated systems which make claiming simple and fast. But, said Tonkery, quality control in claiming is lost or forgotten. Much discussion followed these comments. Several librarians indicated that they adjust their system's automatic prediction as needed to avoid premature or unnecessary claims and that they carefully review claims before sending them out.

John Merriman remarked that his firm is receiving increasing numbers of computer-generated "sweep through" claims and has hired more staff to handle them, only to find that a great number are not legitimate claims.

Tonkery noted that serials departments with automated systems are frequently short-staffed and unable to review automatic claims.

Agents, in turn, do not have staff to review the increased number of claims coming in and may forward them without review to the publisher. Since so few are legitimate claims, the publisher may ignore all of them, and the result is an overall decline in the quality of service.

Several workshop participants suggested that it should be the role of the agent to communicate these problems to individual libraries and to work with the libraries to achieve a reasonable claiming program so that good service can be provided.

A number of factors may affect service charges in the future. Tonkery reported that increases will occur because of the decline in publisher discounts to the agent, increased agent operating costs, changes in title mix, decrease in competitors, and increasing service demands. For instance, publisher's list price will cease to be the exclusive pricing standard. The publications of society and nonprofit publishers, which traditionally offer no discounts to agents, will be billed with an extra fee and will no longer be supported by commercial publications offered at a discount.

Agents will unbundle services. Each service (such as claiming and management reports) will be priced separately. There will be a move by agents to price each library on a cost-recovery basis. Finally, service charges will be determined on a per title basis.

During the discussion period, John Merriman explained that Blackwell's has worked cooperatively with British publishers to set subscription prices early and avoid additional charges. He also explained that, unlike the book trade, there are no bulk discounts in the subscription industry. Another topic was the difficulty experienced by agents and libraries in dealing with fulfillment houses. Fulfillment houses, which are increasingly being used by publishers to distribute journals, are set up to handle address changes and collect money. They do not keep back issues and cannot provide them when claimed.

Workshop participants ended the session on a note of hope for future discussions and cooperation between librarians, agents, and publishers.

Serials Automation – Before, During and After

Linda Marie Golian
Stella Pilling
Virginia R. Reed

Workshop Leaders

Deborah Sommer

Recorder

This workshop focused on serials automation from the planning process to implementation and post-automation, in small, medium, and large libraries, respectively.

Virginia R. Reed, Periodicals Librarian at the Ronald Williams Library, Northeastern Illinois University, Chicago, described the planning phase of serials automation, based on her experience in planning for the implementation of the Innovacq system. Her library has used Innovacq since 1987 for its 3,000 current and 6,000 non-current serials.

As a beginning point, Reed suggested determining which manual files already in the library are actually used and should be transferred to the automated file. After surveying files and consulting with staff, project leaders can create a record template containing all the data actually needed for conversion of each title. If bibliographic data are to be keyed as part of the conversion, it is important to define ahead of time the "standard" bibliographic record and the fields that will be needed in the online system.

As the other speakers observed, Reed noted that while automation will not solve all production problems, automation may enable

---

Deborah Sommer is Head of Periodicals, University of California, Berkeley, CA 94720.

a library to perform new tasks or functions. The general volatility that accompanies automation may also allow the introduction of non-automation changes (for example, space renovation) that serve to support staff morale. Reed concluded with the wry reminder that there is always the next system to plan for!

Linda Marie Golian, Serials Control Librarian at the University of Miami Law Library, Coral Gables, has used the Innovacq system since 1985. She began her discussion of the implementation phase of serials automation by dismissing some common myths regarding serials automation, for example, that automation makes the work much easier and results in staff reductions. She noted that, on the contrary, computers require greater analytical skills and stable staffing levels. She reviewed some ideas for preplanning activities, including a time-and-motion study of serials operations that she conducted. She also offered practical tips for motivating operational staff (for example, do not hide the system's flaws or exaggerate its benefits) during the implementation phase.

Golian emphasized the importance of establishing priorities in the ongoing work during serials automation in order to facilitate processing at a time when demands on staff are very heavy. She observed that statistics can be helpful in determining the most opportune time to begin an automation project and in assessing which processing tasks can be postponed or delayed if necessary. As a result of her analysis, her institution hired a filing services consultant to handle 1,500 looseleaf titles and also reduced binding and new subscriptions for one year. She cautioned managers to be ruthless about their own time—to set aside some interrupted work time daily—and to delegate some job responsibilities in order to build staff morale and confidence. Finally, Golian urged managers not to forget the human touch and to develop the talents and skills of the staff.

Stella Pilling, Head of the Marketing and Publishing Section of Serial Acquisitions, at The British Library Document Supply Centre, Boston Spa, England, presented the final workshop session on post-implementation of serials automation. The British Library Document Supply Centre (BLDSC) houses 56,000 current and 150,000 non-current serial titles. The Centre supports a major national and international interlibrary lending service, receiving more than 3 million requests each year; the majority of these requests are for serials. Most of the Centre's 800 staff work with serials, and almost two thirds of its budget (almost £ million) are spent on serials.

The Centre's serials automation program has been in existence for almost 25 years. The program began with punched cards and has since evolved its own in-house automated system, since there is no commercially-available system large enough for BLDSC's collection. Pilling described the recent automation of the Centre's check-in ("accessioning") function, which before automation used Kalamazoo binders. She noted that this evolutionary approach to system design may result in a disjointed, non-integrated product.

During implementation of automated serials check-in, the worst problem encountered was the initial slow system response time. The popularity of the new system resulted in unanticipated pressure on the system from non-serials queries. Once the new check-in system was implemented, the Centre maintained parallel manual and automated check-in for one month, giving staff a chance to practice using the new system and to make mistakes without risking data loss.

Pilling echoed Golian in stating the importance of making one's own timetable for implementation, if possible. In addition, there is great pressure on the manager who may be simultaneously responsible for maintaining operations, engaging in training activities, performing routine personnel tasks, and trouble-shooting, while managing the automation project. Pilling concluded by emphasizing the importance of putting the personal side, rather than the technical, first during an automation project.

Several areas of common concern emerged among the speakers. All speakers stressed the importance of good personnel management during the planning and implementation process, and offered a variety of methods to support and motivate staff who are coping with change in the workplace. The successful engagement of staff in the process of automation is a measure of project success. The political environment in the institution also has an impact on the process of serials automation, from the initial selection of a system through organizational changes growing out of automation.

The issue of changes in classification level of operational staff following automation prompted lively discussion during the question-and-answer period. Golian and Pilling reported the upgrading of operational staff because of increased need for problem-solving and analytical skills, while Reed reported the creation of a new position for computer input. Participants and audience also discussed how to handle current check-in during the implementation of automation.

The Subscription Agent and the Integrated Library Systems Vendor: A Marriage Made in Heaven?

Sharon Cline McKay
Frederick E. Schwartz

Workshop Leaders

Constance L. Foster

Recorder

Fritz Schwartz, Manager of Electronic Data Interchange Services, The Faxon Company, and Sharon Cline McKay, Director of Library Services, EBSCO Subscription Services, provided an informal and interactive approach to the complex topic of the relationship between the integrated library systems (ILS) vendor and the subscription agent in the development of interfaces. Schwartz introduced the topic by describing this relationship as a triangular one involving three key players: ILS vendor, subscription agent, and library. Before exploring specific issues and future concerns, Schwartz guided participants through definitions of standards, systems terminology, significant acronyms, and key words in electronic communications. He stressed the importance of librarians becoming familiar and conversant with the data processing environment and linked systems.

Schwartz then posed the question of why we want to link systems in the library world. Answers included improved accuracy of data entry; elimination of redundant input; increased processing speed; reduction in manual labor costs; consistent formats; links for trading

---

Constance L. Foster is Serials Supervisor, Western Kentucky University, Bowling Green, KY 42101-3576.

© 1990 by The Haworth Press, Inc. All rights reserved.

partners; and as one participant added, the best of all systems linked together, or integrated functionality.

To continue, Schwartz considered what kind of information about serials we want to exchange electronically. He offered numerous examples such as MARC and non-MARC bibliographic and holdings records, publication patterns, invoices, claims, purchase orders, cancellations, bindery information, price lists; rather futuristic needs such as transmission of sound, graphics, holographs; and more immediately, full text and citations. An addition to this list was the need for various management reports. Publication patterns drew the most discussion as a definite priority within the serials community. Schwartz concluded that librarians should continue to make known their needs to ILS vendors and agents so that useful developments and refinements can occur.

Next, Sharon Cline McKay detailed the steps that an ILS vendor takes in developing an interface. Beginning with a client "reference" interview, the ILS vendor and often the serials subscription agent discuss what the mutual client really wants. At that point, the vendor creates a plan, reviews available standards, assesses system capabilities, and writes specifications, which are then reviewed by all parties. According to McKay, testing, documentation, analysis, pricing, marketing, release of the interface, possible training needs, use, and planned discontinuance complete the process. She stressed that subscription agents must work with the ILS vendors to create a feasible exchange of ideas, but that the technical aspects of an interface rest with systems staff.

To illustrate the complexity of such interaction, Schwartz assisted McKay by drawing a grid on the chalkboard with vertical representation for role, cost, and benefit, and a horizontal listing of the players in this relationship. In addition to the three major players, McKay identified others such as a bibliographic utility, publisher, local computer center, fulfillment center, campus accounting center, and bindery. Schwartz noted that any given player can fill several roles at one time, thereby increasing the complexity of the process. The client librarian, however, may not always understand how much the ILS vendor can actually accomplish within this intricate relationship.

Moving to practical advice, McKay suggested that librarians can become effective players by staying informed abut the interface process and the roles of other participants. She advised librarians to maintain reasonable expectations when formulating requests for proposals and to become actively involved in setting standards. Since over forty formats are currently used for transmitting business documents, McKay and Schwartz both underscored the importance of standards. Even locally, if a library adheres to consistent methods of encoding any data, then a shift to standardized formats—a new ILS system, upgrade of existing ones, or maintenance of two versions simultaneously—will not be nearly as difficult or labor-intensive as in a situation where inconsistency reigns.

McKay cautioned that any ILS vendor wants to see convincing benefits before the vendor will reorder priorities for its clients. The subscription agent cannot always push for enhancements; the client, therefore, must often assume responsibility by lobbying, becoming involved in the standards setting process, and by writing reasonable requirements into contracts and proposals. She also encouraged flexibility and good nature for all concerned.

In concluding the workshop, McKay presented points to consider in ILS vendor selection. Financial stability, technical currency, familiarity and compliance with data processing standards (both within the library community and in the larger setting of the business world), professional ability of the design and support staff, vendor experience, and flexibility and appropriateness of services to customers all support a viable ILS vendor/subscription agent/client relationship.

Schwartz added that the foremost problem in data exchange today is the lack of adequate standards, coupled with no clear time frame and a sense of urgency on the part of those involved in this particular issue. Many ILS vendors view serials as the "last frontier" and an unimportant subsystem of the total ILS package. Schwartz and McKay agreed that realistic expectations, seeking information about relevant aspects of data exchange, and involvement in addressing and resolving important issues are three factors that will move all players forward in this significant, yet costly, effort to maintain effective relationships in the development of interfaces.

The Thor Inventory Ruling: Fact or Fiction?

Marcia Anderson
Don Jaeger
Lenore Wilkas

Workshop Leaders

Margaret McKinley

Recorder

In 1979, the Supreme Court ruled against the Thor Power Tool Company, stating that ". . . no longer could any producer—whether tool manufacturer or publisher—write down the value of inventoried goods to decrease taxes on profits."[1] The effect of the Thor ruling on publishers and the implications for libraries and vendors were the subject of this workshop.

Don Jaeger, Vice President of Alfred Jaeger, Inc., opened the workshop by reporting on his literature search. He examined the literature for discussions of the effect of the Thor ruling for libraries and publishers. Initially, libraries' fears of mass book destruction appeared to be realized when Plenum Press destroyed over 322,000 books in order to claim a tax deduction. Later, however, publishers successfully promoted legislation to exempt publishers from a 1979 tax payback of inventories.

Jaeger explained that, under the Thor ruling, publishers may not take a tax deduction unless their stock is destroyed or reduced in price. The consequences of this ruling for publishers depends on the accounting method used to evaluate inventories. Publishers using the "last in, first out" (LIFO) method were not affected by the

Margaret McKinley is Head of the Serials Department, University Research Library, University of California, Los Angeles, CA 90024.

ruling since inventories of back issues or monographs are based on the cost of the latest item to enter the inventory, thereby reducing profits. Publishers who were affected used the "first in, first out" (FIFO) method, basing inventory value on the cost of the earliest item in the inventory, thereby increasing profits. FIFO is good for stockholder reports but bad for tax returns. Some publishers using the FIFO method destroyed most of their inventory. Some used different inventory accounting methods for books and periodicals, so that periodical issues were kept but books were sold.

The Tax Reform Act of 1987 had further implications for publishers. Because the tax rate for large corporations was lowered, publishers found it unnecessary to attempt to reduce their taxes further by adjusting their inventories.

Reporting on 30 interviews with publishers and vendors, Jaeger noted that print runs for journals and books have been reduced. One publishers "pulps" excess journal volumes at the end of the year and transfers the rest to a subsidiary company for sale. Two back issues dealers believe that their back issue fulfillment rates from publishers range between 50 and 60 percent. Not-for-profit publishers are not subject to taxation and may, therefore, have longer print runs and warehouse more issues. One major academic publisher observed that there was a small reduction in the number of back issue orders they were able to fill. This publisher reported smaller print runs, higher unit costs, more unfulfilled orders, earlier remaindering, and a great need for reprinting.

Lenore Wilkas, Serials Acquisitions Librarian at the University of Pennsylvania, described her experience in ordering replacements direct from publishers. She stated that there was a 90 percent fulfillment rate for replacement issues ordered from publishers and an 85-90 percent rate for direct back volume orders.

Wilkas made several observations about direct replacement orders. Suppliers often send pro forma invoices in response to Penn's orders. In general, it is more difficult to replace low to moderately priced journal issues than to replace expensive issues. Ordering replacements and back volumes from publishers had increased the number of invoices the library handles and also results in an increased number of publisher mistakes. Wilkas believes that the University of Pennsylvania's experience in ordering direct from publishers was positive.

Marci Anderson, Head of the Acquisitions Department at Arizona State University, reported on the ASU experience with ordering replacements from vendors. She stated that the availability of online holdings statements at ASU makes identification of missing issues simple, but that the issues themselves are becoming more difficult to acquire. Until 1989, ASU sent letters inquiring as to price and availability of back issues and also sent several follow-ups. If there was no response to the follow-ups, orders were sent in succession to Universal Serials & Book Exchange (USBE), library selectors for review, and then to a single issues dealer.

ASU staff analyzed forty-eight orders that had been outstanding for up to three years. Of these, 67 percent had been ordered within two years of publication and 28 percent were prepaid. A total of thirty-eight orders were filled by publishers. The staff at ASU noted that back issues are now less available. The number of prepaid orders has increased. The number of unfilled orders has increased, including prepaids. The cost of replacements and especially back volumes has increased.

ASU has recently revised its procedures. The staff send first and second claims for missing issues earlier. In ordering replacements, ASU now sends an authorization to ship and bill if price and shipping charges do not exceed a certain amount. ASU also orders from dealers earlier in the replacement process.

Discussion among attendees at the workshop centered around procedures for replacing missing issues. Online files of major serials vendors have proved helpful in locating publisher addresses. Librarians also order missing issues through serials vendors. Telephone follow-up for firm orders has been effective in increasing the fulfillment rate, although there was agreement that original orders should be printed.

In responding to Wilkas' remarks about problems with publisher orders, a publisher's representative in the audience remarked that errors in fulfilling back issue orders are high because of minimal staff training. Publishers require prepayment because institutions frequently do not pay these invoices. Moreover, there is a high rate of return.

Subsequent remarks during the discussion revealed that factors in addition to the Thor Ruling are affecting the cost and supply of back issues of journals. Because information is now disseminated in many different formats, there is not as much demand for paper materials. Publishers are making journal articles available in electronic format before issues are published. There may be a five percent variance in the print run of a journal. If a print run is low and if there are also problems with mailing bags or labels, the number of issues available to fill replacement orders may be far lower than the publisher had anticipated.

NOTE

1. Thor Power Tool Co. v. C.I.R., 439 U.S. 522 (1979).

Fourth Annual NASIG Conference Registrants, Scripps College, June 1989

Conference Registrants	Institution
Aiello, Helen M.	Wesleyan University
Alan, Robert	University of California/San Diego
Alessi, Dana L.	Baker & Taylor
Alexander, Adrian W.	The Faxon Company
Alexander, Julie S.	University of Texas/Arlington
Allerhand, Lorraine	University of Southern California
Amann, Elizabeth	Swarthmore College
Anderson, Anthony E.	University of Southern California
Anderson, Jan	Utah State University
Anderson, Marcia	Arizona State University
Arcand, Janet	Iowa State University
Astle, Deana L.	Clemson University
Aufdemberge, Karen	University of Toledo
Baigent, Pattie	EBSCO Subscription Services
Baker, Carol M.	Canadian Institute for Scientific and Technical Information
Baker, Mary Ellen	California Polytechnic State University
Baldwin, Jane	North Carolina State University
Barbour, Wendell	Christopher Newport College
Barker, Caroline J.	Florida International University
Barnes, Ilse E.	University of West Florida

Barnes, Roy	University of Toledo
Baron, Joel	The Faxon Company
Barry, Jane	Nassau Community College
Basch, Buzzy	EBSCO Subscription Services
Bergholz, Donna Chapin	Duke University
Born, Kathleen	EBSCO Subscription Services
Boss, Valerie	California Polytechnic State University
Bourquin, David	California State University
Braden, Jim W., Jr.	Georgia State University
Braden, Mark	Occidental College
Bradley, Melissa B.	Denver Public Library
Brannon, Mary K.	Louisiana State University
Breedlore, Rebecca	University of Massachusetts/Boston
Breton, Gabriel	National Library of Canada
Broadway, Rita	Memphis State University
Brooks, Howard	Scripps College
Brown-May, Patricia A.	University of Michigan/Dearborn
Brugger, Judy	City College, City University of New York
Buell, Vivian	Ballen Booksellers International
Busic, Zdravka A.	Oberlin College
Bustion, Marifran	Texas A & M University
Callaghan, Jean	Wheaton College
Cap, Maria	University of Southern California
Carboni, Cheryl	National Library of Canada
Carlson, Melvin, Jr.	University of Massachusetts/Amherst
Carrington, Bradley D.	Northwestern University
Case, Mary M.	Northwestern University
Castle, Mary K.	University of Texas/Arlington
Chadwick, Leroy	University of Washington
Champagne, Thomas E.	University of Illinois/Urbana
Chang, Chia-Ching	Bucknell University

Chang, Min-min	California Institute of Technology
Chao, Theresa	University of Wisconsin/ Stevens Point
Chatterton, Leigh A.	Nelinet, Inc.
Christianson, Inelda	Loma Linda University
Churukian, Araxie	University of California/ Riverside
Clack, Mary Elizabeth	Harvard College
Clark, Stephen D.	College of William and Mary
Clay, Genevieve	Eastern Kentucky University
Clifton, James	*New England Journal of Medicine*
Coats, Jacqueline	University of Chicago
Cohen, David	College of Charleston
Coleman, Earl M.	EMCE
Collins, Dorothy	Boley International Subscription Agency
Cook, Eleanor I.	North Carolina State University
Courtney, Keith	Taylor & Francis, Ltd.
Cousineau, Marie	University of Ottawa
Coyle, Marian	Martinus Nijhoff International
Cresto, Kathy	Thousand Oaks Library
Crump, Michele	Stanford University
Cummins, Lynn M.	California State University/ Northridge
Curtis, Jerry	Springer-Verlag
Czech, Isabel	Institute for Scientific Information
D'Andraia, Dana	University of California
Dabkowski, Charles	Niagara University
Dane, Stephen M.	Kluwer Academic Publishers
Darling, Karen	University of Oregon
Davis, Susan	State University of New York/ Buffalo
Dawson, Julie Eng	Princeton Theological Seminary

Day, Nancy	Linda Hall Library
DeRouen, Jimi	ABC-CLIO
Degener, Christie T.	University of North Carolina/Chapel Hill
Dicaire, Raymond	University of Ottawa
Doescher, Starla	University of the Pacific
Douglass, Janet	Texas Christian University
Duffek, Elizabeth	Air Force Geophysics Library
Dykstra, Stephanie	University of British Columbia
Ebersole, Brian	Libraries of the Claremont Colleges
Echt, Rita	Michigan State University
Edelman, Marla	University of North Carolina/Greensboro
Ennerberg, Erik	California State Polytechnic University/Pomona
Fairley, Craig	Metro Toronto Reference Library
Feick, Tina	Blackwell's
Field, Kenneth	Trent University
Finerty, Michele	Orange County Law Library
Foster, Constance L.	Western Kentucky University
Foulke, Phyllis	Cardinal Stritch College
Frye, Betty George E.	University of South Carolina
Fulsaas, Esther	University of California/Berkeley
Gartrell, Joyce	Columbia University
Geer-Butler, Beverley	George Washington University
Gelenter, Win	National Agricultural Library
Geller, Marilyn	Massachusetts Institute of Technology
Gianakos, Bessie	Libraries of the Claremont Colleges
Gladish, Wayne	California State University/Los Angeles
Glasgow, Kay	State University of New York/Binghamton
Goforth, Kathleen	Academic Book Center

Golian, Linda Marie	University of Miami
Gordon, Martin	Franklin and Marshall College
Gormley, Alice	Marquette University
Graham, Henrietta P.	Atlanta-Fulton Public Library
Graves, Shirley	Loma Linda University
Grover, Diane	University of Washington
Gunter, Linda	Libraries of the Claremont Colleges
Gurshman, Sandra J.	Baker & Taylor
Hall, Phyllis	Pergamon Press, Inc.
Hamilton, Lisanne	Trident Technical College
Hanks, Nancy	Slippery Rock University
Haripersad, Indira	University of Alberta
Harris, Jay	University of Alabama
Hartman, Anne-Marie	Queens College, City University of New York
Hartman, Matthew	University of British Columbia
Hashert, Cynthia	University of Texas/Arlington
Hayman, Lynne	EBSCO Subscription Services
Helms, Mary E.	Washington University
Hemmert, Mary Ella	University of Southern California
Hénon, Alain	University of California Press
Hepfer, Cindy	*Serials Review*
Heroux, Marlene Sue	EBSCO Subscription Services
Hogan, Kathleen	University of Calgary
Holley, Beth	University of Alabama
Horvath, Steve	Sage Periodicals Press
Hsia, Ting-Mei	California State Polytechnic University/Pomona
Hsieh, Jennifer	University of Massachusetts
Hurley, Jamie	The Faxon Company
Irvin, Judy	Louisiana Technical University
Ito, Mary E.	California Institute of Technology
Ivins, October	Louisiana State University
Jacobsen, Bruce	Bridgeport National Bindery

Jaeger, Don	Alfred Jaeger, Inc.
Jager, Con	Swets Subscription Service
James, Rebecca R.	Baker & Taylor
Johnson, Ben	EBSCO Subscription Services
Johnson, Brent	University of Alberta
Johnson, Jane G.	Georgia Southern College
Jones, Daniel H.	University of Texas
Juhl, Beth	Columbia University
Kalmerton, Phyllis	Palmer College of Chiropractic
Karasick, Alice W.	University of Southern California
Kean, Gene	Allen Press, Inc.
Keating, Lawrence R., II	University of Houston
Kellogg, Martha H.	University of Rhode Island
Kennedy, Kit	Coutts Library Services, Inc.
Kerr, Linda	University of Alberta
Kidder, Audrey J.	Wright State University
Kim, Kumsun	California State University/Fullerton
Kinell, Susan K.	ABC-CLIO
Kirkland, Kenneth	DePaul University
Kleindienst, Juedi S.	North Carolina Central University
Knapp, Leslie	EBSCO Subscription Services
Krishan, K.	University of Saskatchewan
Krissiep, Margot	Washington State University
Kropf, Blythe	New York Public Library
Kwan, Cecilia	University of California/Davis
Lai, Sheila	California State University/Sacramento
Lakhanpal, S. K.	University of Saskatchewan
Landesman, Margaret	University of Utah
Landry, Melinda	Southern California Edison Company
Lane, Alice	University of Nebraska
Lange, Janice	Sam Houston State University
Leach, Travis	University of Arizona
Leachman, Chuck	EBSCO Subscription Services

Leazer, William V.	Majors Scientific Subscriptions
Lenzini, Rebecca T.	Carl Systems, Inc.
Levin, Fran	Houston Public Library
Lightbody, Melanie W.	University of Washington
Lim, Sue	California State Polytechnic University/Pomona
Lindsay, Robin D.	Furman University
Llewellyn, Anthony J.	Butterworths
Lohnes, Dick	EBSCO Subscription Services
Long, Maurice	*British Medical Journal*
Lutz, Linda	University of Western Ontario
MacAdam, Carol	Princeton University
Maddox, Jane	Otto Harrassowitz
Magenau, Carol	Dartmouth College
Malinowski, Teresa	California State University/Fullerton
Markley, Susan	Villanova University
Markwith, Michael	The Faxon Company
Marshall, Sharon	University of Alberta
Mason, Armanda	University of California/Berkeley
Mauldin, Ellen	Mississippi State University
McAdam, Tim	Boston College
McBride, Donna	Boston Public Library
McCalla, Anna	Trent University
McCalla, Doug	Trent University
McCammon, Leslie V.	Florida International University
McCann, Kristine	McGregor Subscription Service
McCune, David	Sage Publications
McCune, Sara	Sage Publications
McCutcheon, Dianne	National Library of Medicine
McDonough, Joyce	University of Louisville
McGarry, Dorothy	University of California/Los Angeles
McGrath, Kathleen	University of British Columbia

McKay, Peter	Harcourt Brace Jovanovich, Ltd.
McKay, Sharon Cline	EBSCO Subscription Services
McKinley, Margaret	University of California/ Los Angeles
Meiseles, Linda	Brooklyn College
Meneely, Kathleen	Cleveland Health Sciences Library
Menzel, Daniel	*Toxicology Letters*
Merbaum, Mark	University of Southern California
Mering, Margaret V.	University of Colorado
Merriman, John	Blackwell's
Merryman, Peggy	U.S. Geological Survey Library
Meyle, Joyce	AMOCO Corporation
Michalak, Joseph	SilverPlatter
Moles, Jean Ann	University of Arkansas
Montanary, Barbara	University of California
Mooers, M. Jeanne	Naval Ocean Systems Center
Moore, Patricia	Michigan University
Morgano, Susan M.	Alfred Jaeger, Inc.
Mueller, Britt K.	University of Oregon
Mueller, Carolyn J.	Humboldt State University
Muhammad, Suad	University of Arizona
Murphy, Pency	Texas Instruments, Inc.
Myers, Carolyn W.	Duke University
Napier, Pat	Napier Polytechnic of Edinburgh
Narayanan, Kamala S.	Queen's University
Nason, Stanley	Readmore Publications, Inc.
Nissley, Meta	California State University/ Chico
Noda, Nancy	San Francisco State University
Nordlie, Kris	CLSI, Inc.
O'Neill, Rosanna M.	OCLC, Inc.
Ogburn, Joyce L.	The Pennsylvania State University
Okerson, Ann	Jerry Alper, Inc.

Osheroff, Shiela Keil	Oregon State University
Page, Gillian	Pageant Publishing
Palm, Miriam	Stanford University
Parang, Elizabeth	University of Nevada/ Las Vegas
Parker, Laura	Elsevier Science Publishing Company, Inc.
Patrick, Carol	Cleveland State University
Pearce, Linda	University of Calgary
Pender, Maureen Jenkins	Faxon Canada, Ltd.
Peterson, Lisa	University of California
Phillips, Sharon	California State University/ Hayward
Piesbergen, Frances	University of Missouri/ St. Louis
Pilling, Stella	British Library Document Supply Center
Pionessa, Geraldine F.	University of Arizona
Polakoff, Paul	University of Southern California
Polson, Lin	Simon Fraser University
Popkin, Richard	*Journal of the History of Philosophy*
Porter, Sherry	Texas College of Osteopathic Medicine
Postlethwaite, Bonnie	The Faxon Company
Presley, Roger L.	Georgia State University
Putney, Patricia	Brown University
Quigg, Agnes	University of Hawaii
Radencich, John	Florida International University
Raines, M. Diane	Dynix, Inc. Automated Systems
Rains, Gina E.	Burroughs Wellcome Company
Ralston, M. Joan	Villanova University
Randall, Michael H.	University of California/ Los Angeles

Rankin, Juliann E.	California State University/Chico
Rast, Elaine	Northern Illinois University
Reed, Joy	University Microfilms International
Reed, Virginia R.	Northeastern Illinois University
Reich, Vicky	Stanford University
Ribbe, Paul	Virginia Polytechnic Institute and State University
Rice, Patricia Ohl	The Pennsylvania State University
Richey, Debora	California State University
Riddick, John F.	Central Michigan University
Rieke, Judith L.	Vanderbilt University
Riley, Cheryl	Central Missouri State University
Robischon, Rose	United States Military Academy
Robnett, Bill	Rice University
Rogers, Marilyn L.	University of Arkansas
Rogers, Nancy H.	EBSCO Subscription Services
Romanick, Charlotte	Butterworth Publishers
Rossignol, Lucien R.	Smithsonian Institution
Rossini, Adriana	University of Toronto
Roth, Dana	California Institute of Technology
Sahak, Judy Harvey	Libraries of the Claremont Colleges
Santosuosso, Joe	The Faxon Company
Saxe, Minna C.	City University of New York
Sayler, Terry Ann	University of Maryland
Scanlan, Brian	Elsevier Science Publishing Company, Inc.
Scanland, Roger	University of Arizona
Scarry, Patricia	University of Chicago Press
Schaafsma, Carol	University of Hawaii
Schleifer, Harold B.	California State Polytechnic University/Pomona

Schuneman, Anita	University of Illinois
Schuster, Jack H.	Claremont Graduate School
Schwartz, Fredrick	Faxon Electronic Data
Schwartz, Holly	Cleveland Health Sciences Library
Schwartzkopf, Becky	Mankato State University
Scott, Sharon K.	University of Arizona
Scullin, Jan	Massachusetts General Hospital
Seale, Linda N.	University of Alberta
Sederstrom, Gene	University of South Dakota
Sell, Mary Grace	The Faxon Company
Settle, Huguette	University of Alberta
Sexton, Ebba Jo	University of Kentucky
Shaffer, Barbara	University of Toledo
Shaw, Deborah L.	Oklahoma State University
Shelton, Judith M.	Georgia State University
Sherer, Ree	EBSCO Subscription Services
Shroyer, Andrew	University of California/Santa Barbara
Siever, Arlene M.	Indiana University–Purdue University
Silverman, Karen Sandlin	PALINET
Silverman, Scott H.	Bryn Mawr College
Sleep, Esther L.	Brock University
Smith, Jeanne L.	Xerox Corporation
Smith, Martha Eszes	Libraries of the Claremont Colleges
Smithers, Anne S.	University of Alberta
Somers, Sally W.	University of Georgia
Sommer, Deborah	University of California/Berkeley
Soper, Mary Ellen	University of Washington
Soupiset, Kathy	Trinity University
Sowa, Kathryn	New Mexico State University
Stapleton, Diana L.	Eastern Kentucky University
Steele, Heather	Blackwell's
Steinhagen, Elizabeth N.	University of Idaho
Stensvold, Chris	Thousand Oaks Library

Stern, Gillian	Sage Publications, Ltd.
Stover, Sarah	University of Southern California
Sturgeon, Susan	Salem State College
Su, Julie	Indiana University–Purdue University
Sullivan, Eugene	University of South Alabama
Sutherland, Laurie	University of Washington
Szeto, Dorcas C.	Azusa Pacific University
Tagler, John	Elsevier Science Publishing Company, Inc.
Talley, Kaye	University of Central Arkansas
Tallman, Karen	University of Arizona
Teaster-Woods, Gale	Winthrop College
Tenney, Joyce	University of Maryland/ Baltimore
Terry, Martha Nancy	Grand Valley State University
Thomas, David	Michigan Technological University
Thomas, Evelyne B.	Davidson College
Thompson, Jacqueline	John Wiley and Sons
Thompson, James	University of California
Thompson, Sherry L.	Majors Scientific Subscriptions
Thornberry, Pat	University of South Florida
Thorne, Kathleen	San Jose State University
Thornton, Chris	Case Western Reserve University
Thyden, Wayne	EBSCO Subscription Services
Tiffany, Bill	Memorial University of Newfoundland
Timmons, Sarah S.	Wright State University
Tonkery, Dan	Readmore Publications, Inc.
Tribit, Donald K.	Millersville University
Tseng, Sally C.	University of California/Irvine
Turitz, Mitch	San Francisco State University
Tuttle, Marcia	University of North Carolina/ Chapel Hill

Van Goethem, Jeri	Duke University
Van Tong, Dieu	University of Alabama/ Birmingham
VanAssche Bueter, Rita	Blackwell North America, Inc.
Vanderhoof, Audrey	Texas Christian University
Vent, Marilyn	University of Nevada/ Las Vegas
Waldman, Nancy	Sprague Library
Walker, Alberta	Libraries of the Claremont Colleges
Walker, Elaine	Cornell University
Wall, Colleen	3M Company
Wallace, Patricia M.	University of Northern Colorado
Wang, Anna	Ohio State University
Ward, David R.	Louisiana State University
Ward, Jeannette	University of Central Florida
Weaver, Sandy	Innovative Interfaces
Wechselberg, Irene	University of California/Irvine
Weed, Joe K.	EBSCO Subscription Services
Weed, Merry	Springer-Verlag
Weller, Ann C.	University of Illinois/Chicago
Wharton, Patrick	Kluwer Academic Publishers
White, Myra	California State Polytechnic University/Pomona
Wilkas, Lenore R.	University of Pennsylvania
Wilkerson, Judy	University of Texas Southwestern Medical Center
Williams, Geraldine	Northern Kentucky University
Williams, Kristine	University of Alberta
Williams, Linda F.	Northern Arizona University
Williams, Susan	University of Colorado
Willmering, Bill	National Library of Medicine
Winchester, David	Washburn University
Winjum, Roberta	University of Missouri/ Columbia

Wirtz, Theresa	Yankee Book Peddler
Woodward, Hazel	Loughborough University
Yuster, Leigh C.	R. R. Bowker
Zager, Pamela	Lamar University

Index

AACR. *See* Anglo-American Cataloging Rules
ABC-CLIO, 172
Abstracts, 44-45,47
Academic libraries. *See also* names of specific libraries
  vendor bidding by, 175
Acquisitions, cooperative, 167-168
Against the Grain, 108,147
AGRICOLA, on CD-ROM, 53
American Association for the Advancement of Science, 18,118-119
American Chemical Society, Petroleum Research Fund, 126,130
American Council of Learned Societies, 118-119
American Historical Review, 29
American Institute of Physics, 109
American Journal of Science, 124,134,135
American Library Association (ALA), 109-110,159
American Library Association Cataloging Rules, 155
American Medical Association, 146
American Mineralogist, 130,133,135,141
American Physical Society, 18
American Professor (Schuster), 16
Anglo-American Cataloging Rules, 155
Anglo-American Cataloging Rules 2, 156
Arizona State University Library, 193
Association of American Universities, 118-119
Association of Research Libraries (ARL)
  serials department survey, 159
  serials pricing studies, 110,111-119
    Economic Consulting Services Inc, report, 111-113,151
    Okerson report, 110,113-119
Authorship, multiple, 20-21

Automated serials systems, 183-186

Back issues, 192,193. *See also* Missing issues, claiming of
Bibliographic citations. *See* Citations
Bibliographic instruction programs, 65
Bibliographic records. *See also* Citations
  in automation conversion, 183
Bidding, for subscription service, 175-187
Binding, 153-154
BITNET, 108
Blackwell Scientific Publications, Ltd., 134,181
Books in Print Plus, on CD-ROM, 52
Bowen, Howard R., 16
R.R. Bowker, 52
British Library Document Supply Centre, 184-185
Browsing, 2,9
BRS, 45,50,172
BRS After Dark, 63
  on CD-ROM, 73,74
Budget, serials analysis and, 168
Bulletin de Minéralogie, 135
Business Periodicals Index, on CD-ROM, 53

California Institute of Technology, 172
Canadian Library Association, 109
Canadian Mineralogist, 135
Catalog
  card, 155-156
  on CD-ROM, 56
  online, 46-48
Cataloging
  with CD-ROM CATCD 450, 56
  of CD-ROM products, 77

© 1989 by The Haworth Press, Inc. All rights reserved.   209

latest entry, 155-157
 of non-print serials, 164
 of software, 164
CD-ROM, 49-62, 69-80
 bibliographic citation standards, 164
 Columbia University Libraries study,
   69-80
 cost, 63, 64, 72, 76-77, 147, 163-164
 disadvantages, 75, 76, 77
 hard copy versus, 57-59, 61, 71-72, 74-76
 indexes, 45-46, 149
 interlibrary loan and, 65, 66-67, 75
 librarians' evaluation of, 74-76
 literature searching with, 52, 59, 63-67
   cost, 63, 64
   online access versus, 61, 73-74
 networking with, 60, 61, 77, 164
 PALINET use of, 49-62
   CD-ACCESS program, 52-56, 57
     funding, 57-58, 60
     hard copy subscriptions versus, 57-59,
       61
     literature searching applications, 59
     technical service products, 56
     trends, 56-59
     union catalog, 56
     vendors, 57, 60-61
 staff response, 65-66
 standard search method, 46, 60-61
 training for, 59-60, 72, 76, 77-78
 users' response, 64-65, 71-74
CD-ROM products, cataloging of, 77
CINAHL, on CD-ROM, 53
Circulation
 as journal prestige indicator, 132-135
 journal pricing and, 5-6, 132, 133-135
Citation analysis, of mineralogical journals,
   122-126
Citations
 CD-ROM standards, 164
 in indexes/abstracts, 44-45, 46-48
 online catalog, 46-48
Clays and Clay Minerals, 135, 136
Coauthorship, 20-21
Cohen, David, 145
Collection analysis, 167-169
Collection development, 145
College of Charleston library, 46-48

Columbia University Libraries, CD-ROM
   study, 69-80
Commercial Binding Agreement, 153-154
Communication, scholarly, 43-44. *See also*
   Journals(s); Publishing, scholarly
 context of, 15-23
   academic specialization and, 16-18
 in the humanities, 25-32
   article refereeship, 27-29
   editor's role, 25-32
   economic factors, 31-32
   obsolescence of, 32
   publication backlog, 29
   unsolicited, 27, 29
 librarian's role, 150
 publisher's role, 150
 in science, 30, 32
*Computer Science in Economics and
   Management*, 146
Contributions to Mineralogy and Petrology,
   134, 136, 141
Copyright, 65
Crow, Trammell, 89
Current Awareness Bulletin for Education,
   171
Current awareness services, 171-173

Database. *See also* names of specific
   databases
 on local computer systems, 45
DATALINX, 108
Data Research Associates, 47
Dayton Acquisition Cooperative, 167-168
Department of Energy, research grants,
   126, 129, 130
Des Savants, 159
DIALOG, 50, 73
 on CD-ROM, 45, 52
 Knowledge Index, 63

EBSCO, 81, 108
EBSCONET, 108
Economic Consulting Services Inc, serials
   pricing study, 111-113, 151
Economic Geology, 134, 135, 136
Editor, of humanities journals, 25-32

Index

Electronic claim system, 83-84
Electronic journals, 115,173
Electronic library, 173
Electronic mail, 146
Electronic publishing, 38-40,149
Elsevier Scientific Publishers, 110,112-113, 134,149,150-151
ERIC, on CD-ROM, 46,52,53,59,64
European Journal of Mineralogy, 135
Exchange rate, journal prices and, 135-139

Facts on File News Digest, on CD-ROM, 53
Faculty
   library use by, 43-44
   publications of, 18-21
      excessive, 115-116
      indicators of, 19-21
      by junior faculty, 19
      by mid-career faculty, 19-20
      publication rate, 43
      by senior faculty, 19-20
      tenure and, 19,115,146
      by university presses, 35-41
FAX, 146
Faxon, 81
   DATALINX, 108
Fraud, scientific, 20,145,146
Fulfillment houses, 181

GEAC Integrated Library System, 93,95, 96,97
General Science Index, on CD-ROM, 75
Geochemical Journal, 135
Geochimica et Cosmochimica Acta, 132, 135-136

H.W. Wilson, 47,53
   Wilsondisc, 73-74
   WILSONLINE, 50
Hahnemann University Library, CD-ROM use, 63-64
Harrassowitz, 81
Hegel, Georg Wilhelm Friedrich, 30
Heidegger, Martin, 30

Helms, Mary, 149
Henon, Alain, 145-146
Humanities, 43
   scholarly communication in, 25-32
      academic specialization in, 16-18
      article refereeship, 27-29
      economic factors, 31-32
      editor's role, 25-32
      obsolescence of, 32
      publication backlog, 29
      unsolicited, 27,29
Humanities Index, on CD-ROM, 53
Hume, David, 30-31
Hypertext, 163

ICP Software Information Database, on CD-ROM, 53
Immediacy index, of mineralogical journals, 124-126
Impact factors, 2,6
   of mineralogical journals, 124,130-132, 141
Indexes, 44-45
   CD-ROM, 45-46,149
   online, 45-46
Indonesia, journal collections, 10
Inflation, journal prices and, 10-11,112-113
Innovacq system, 183-184
Institute for Scientific Information, 73,172
Interlibrary loan
   by British Library Document Supply Centre, 184-185
   CD-ROM and, 65,66-67,75
International Standard Serials Number (ISSN), 165
Inventory, tax deductions and, 191-192,194
ISSN. *See* International Standard Serials Number

Johns Hopkins University Press, 147
Journal(s). *See also* Serials; names of specific journals
   assessment. *See also* Collection analysis
   cancellation, 106,169
   context of, 1-3
   cost per page, 150-151

electronic, 115,173
funding, 9-10,12-13
impact factors, 2,6,124,130-132,141
mineralogical, 121-142
   assessment tools, 122-130
   circulation, 132-135
   citation analysis, 122-126
   financial support sources, 126-129,
     130,131,132
   immediacy index, 124-126
   impact factors, 124,130-132,141
   prestige assessment, 130-135
   price assessment, 132,133-139,141
   unsupported research and, 129-130
new, 12,13
   evaluation, 169
not-for-profit, 115
online
   browsing and, 9
   cost, 8-9
prestige, 2-3. *See also* Journal(s), impact
   factors
   assessment, 130-135
pricing, 1-13,107-110
   assessment, 132,133-139,141
   Association of Research Libraries
     survey, 110,111-119,151
   circulation relationship, 5-6,132,
     133-135
   currency exchange rate and, 135-139
   inflation and, 10-11,112-113
   library organizations' response,
     109-110
   networking and, 108
   number of pages and, 3,4-5,6
   number of subscribers and, 3-4,5,6
   publishers' profit and, 6-8,113
   publishers' response, 147
   resource sharing and, 173
   of scientific/technical journals,
     111-113,180
   of social science journals, 180
   vendor service charges and, 138-139,
     179-180,181
Journal articles
   acceptance of, 29
   accessing, 43-48,145
   citations. *See* Citations

coauthorship, 20-21
pricing, 9-10,40,145
publication rate, 43
referreed, 2
scientific, 17-18,40
Journal of the History of Philosophy, 29
Journal of Metamorphic Petrology, 134
Journal of Petrology, 134
Juhl, Ruth, 149-150

Kennedy, Kit, 143-144,148,151
Knowledge Index, on CD-ROM, 73,74

Labor market, academic, 21,22
Lanham, Richard, 38-39
Latest Entry Cataloging Rules, 156
LeClerc, Jean, 26,27
Leibniz, Gottfried Wilhelm, 30
Librarians
   CD-ROM evaluation by, 74-76
   scholarly communication role, 150
Library Binding Institute, 154
Library of Congress, 48,109,155
Literature searching. *See also* Online
   searching
   with CD-ROM, 52,59,63-67
   cost, 63,64
   online access versus, 61,73-74
Local Area Network, 77,164
Locke, John, 26

Majors, 81
MARC format/records, 46,47,50-51,82,164
McGregor, 81
Medical Library Association, 109
MEDLINE, on CD-ROM, 52,53,59
Michalak, Joe, 149
Microsoft Bookshelf, on CD-ROM, 53
Mineralogical Magazine, 135,138
Mineralogical Society of America, 121,
   122,141n.
Mineralogical Society of Great Britain,
   138-139
Mineralogy journals. *See* Journal(s),
   mineralogical

Mineralogy and Petrology, 133
Missing issues, claiming of, 103
  electronic systems, 83-84
  fulfillment rate, 192
  publisher-supplied, 82-83,84,192-193
  vendor-supplied, 82-84,180-181,193
MLA, 149
  on CD-ROM, 46,73-74

Napier Polytechnic Library, 171
National Aeronautics and Space Administration (NASA), research grants, 126,129,130
National Institutes of Health, 146
National Library of Canada, 109
National Library of Medicine, 109
National Science Foundation, research grants, 126,127,128,130
Networking
  with CD-ROM, 60,61,77,164
  journal prices and, 108
Newsletter(s), for serials librarians, 159
  serials pricing-related, 109,146-147
Newsletter on Serials Pricing Issues, 109
Newton, Issac, 26-27,30
Nietzsche, Friedrich Wilhelm, 30
North American Serials Interest Group (NASIG), 109,148-149
North Atlantic Treaty Organization (NATO), research grants, 127,129,130
NOTIS, 156
NTIS, on CD-ROM, 53

OCLC, 50,53,160
OCLC Search CD 450 products, 53
Okerson, Ann, 110,113-119
Online searching, 45-46
  CD-ROM versus, 61,73-74
  cost, 73-74
Order consolidation, 93-97,105,147

Page, Gillian, 144,150
PAIS, on CD-ROM, 53
PALINET
  automated services, 50-51
  CD-ROM use, 49-62
    CD-ACCESS program, 53-56,57
    funding, 57-58,60
    hard copy subscriptions versus, 57-59, 61
    literature searching applications, 59
    technical service products, 56
    trends, 56-59
    union catalog, 56
    vendors, 57,60-61
  membership, 50,51
  Microcomputer Support Service Program, 51
  OCLC and, 50
Pennsylvania Area Library Network. *See* PALINET
Pergamon Press, 110,112-113
PERLINE automated serials system, 168-169
Personal computer, 173
Petroleum Research Fund, 126,130
Physics and Chemistry of Minerals, 124, 134,139
Plenum Press, 110,112-113,191
PsychoInfo, on CD-ROM, 73
Psychological Abstracts, on CD-ROM, 64, 66
PsycLIT, on CD-ROM, 53
Publications
  of faculty, 18-21
    excessive, 115-116
    indicators of, 19-21
    by junior faculty, 19
    by mid-career faculty, 19
    publication rate, 43
    by senior faculty, 19-20
    tenure and, 19,115,146
Public libraries, vendor bidding by, 175
Publishers. *See also* names of specific publishers
  inventory-related tax deductions, 191-192,194
  missing issues claiming, 82-83,84, 192-193
  profit of, 6-8,113
  scholarly communication role, 150
Publishing, scholarly

electronic, 38-40,149
by university presses, 35-41

R.R. Bowker, 52
Readers Guide to Periodical Literature, on CD-ROM, 53
Readmore, 81
Refereeing, of journal articles, 27-29
Reich, Vicky, 144-148
Renewal checklist, 106
Research
  funding sources, 126-129,130-132
  journal costs and, 9-10,12-13
Resource sharing, 172-173
Review of Metaphysics, 28,29
Reviews in Mineralogy, 124,133,141-142n.
Ribbe, Paul, 110,145,151

School libraries, vendor bidding by, 175
Schuster, Jack H., 145
Science, scholarly communication in, 30,32
Science Citation Index, on CD-ROM, 73
Science Citation Index Journal Citation Reports, 122-126
SCISEARCH, 172
Selected Water Resource Abstracts, on CD-ROM, 53
Serials
  non-print, 163-164. *See also* CD-ROM
    cataloging of, 164
  title changes, 164-165
Serials department, organizational context, 159-161
Serials Slants, 159
SilverPlatter, 49-50,53
SMARTS, 168
Social Sciences Index, on CD-ROM, 53
Societies, learned, specialization of, 17,18
Society for Scholarly Publishing, 109
Software, cataloging of, 164
Specialization, academic, 16-18,22
Spinoza, Baruch, 30
Springer-Verlag, 110,112-113,117
Staff, automated system implementation by, 184,185-186
Strauch, Katina, 108

Subscription agency. *See* Vendor

Tagler, John, 148-151
Tax deductions, inventory-related, 191-192, 194
Tax Reform Act of 1987, 192
Technical services
  CD-ROM use, 56
  development, 159-160
Tenure, 19,115,146
Thor Inventory ruling, 191-192,194
Title changes, 164-165. *See also*
  Cataloging, latest entry
TOC/DOC current awareness system, 172
Tuttle, Marcia, 108
"Twigging", 134-135

Ulrich's International Periodicals Directory, 17
Ulrich's Plus, on CD-ROM, 52
Union catalog, on CD-ROM, 56
Union Library Catalogue of Pennsylvania, 50
Universal Serials and Book Exchange, 193
University of California Press, 36-38
University of Hawaii Library, 160,161
University of Maryland Library, 160
University of Pennsylvania Library, 192-193
University presses, 35-41,147
  electronic publishing and, 38-40
University of Wisconsin Library, 43-44
Utah State University Library, 93-97

Vendor, 146
  advertising by, 89-91
  bidding for, 175-178
  "boutique". *See* Vendor, specialized services
  of CD-ROM products, 57,60-61
  choice/evaluation, 81-85,100,101-104
    restrictions on, 100-101
  comprehensive services, 81,81-82,87-88, 89
    advantages, 99-100

service charges, 84-85
"department store". *See* Vendor, comprehensive services
integrated library systems, 187-189
missing issues claiming services, 82-84, 180-181, 193
multiple. *See* Vendor, comprehensive services
order consolidation, 93-97, 105, 147
reassignment, 104-106
service charges, 84-85, 102, 179-181

bidding and, 176-177
specialized services, 81, 87-89, 91, 103-105
VU/TEXT, 50

Weiss, Paul, 28, 29
H.W. Wilson, 47, 52
Wilsondisc, 73-74
WILSONLINE, 50
World Bank, 10

For Product Safety Concerns and Information please contact our EU
representative GPSR@taylorandfrancis.com
Taylor & Francis Verlag GmbH, Kaufingerstraße 24, 80331 München, Germany

www.ingramcontent.com/pod-product-compliance
Lightning Source LLC
Chambersburg PA
CBHW052109300426
44116CB00010B/1596